The International Politics of Superheroes

The International Politics of Superheroes

Mariano Turzi

ROWMAN & LITTLEFIELD
Lanham • Boulder • New York • London

Published by Rowman & Littlefield
An imprint of The Rowman & Littlefield Publishing Group, Inc.
4501 Forbes Boulevard, Suite 200, Lanham, Maryland 20706
www.rowman.com

86-90 Paul Street, London EC2A 4NE, United Kingdom

British Library Cataloguing in Publication Information Available

Library of Congress Cataloging-in-Publication Data

Names: Turzi, Mariano, author.
Title: The international politics of superheroes / Mariano Turzi.
Description: Lanham : Rowman & Littlefield Publishing Group, [2022] | Includes bibliographical references and index. | Summary: "This book covers the theories of international relations, pressing current issues, as well as the structures and main players in world politics through the medium of superheroes and supervillains"—Provided by publisher.
Identifiers: LCCN 2021036202 (print) | LCCN 2021036203 (ebook) | ISBN 9781538164945 (cloth) | ISBN 9781538164969 (paperback) | ISBN 9781538164952 (epub)
Subjects: LCSH: International relations—Political aspects. | Superheroes—Social aspects. | Supervillains—Social aspects. | World politics.
Classification: LCC JZ1242 .T87 2022 (print) | LCC JZ1242 (ebook) | DDC 327—dc23/eng/20211105
LC record available at https://lccn.loc.gov/2021036202
LC ebook record available at https://lccn.loc.gov/2021036203

♾ ™ The paper used in this publication meets the minimum requirements of American National Standard for Information Sciences Permanence of Paper for Printed Library Materials, ANSI/NISO Z39.48-1992.

To my WonderWife Gladys Pierpauli, for whom I try to be a superhero every day.
To Felicitas, who wants to be super when she already is.
To Miranda, who has more superpowers than she can imagine.
To Candelaria, who inspired and wrote this book in more ways than she can imagine.

Contents

Preface

For Swiss philosopher Carl Gustav Jung (1959), an archetype is an inherited memory represented in the mind by a universal symbol that is observable in dreams (on an individual level) and in myths (on a collective level). Superheroes are modern archetypes. As present-day myths or modern folktales, they reveal basic truths of human affairs. In this book, I have focused on international affairs. Superheroes constitute—in a sociological sense—heuristic devices: images that I propose simply as aids to analysis, an intellectual strategy for understanding international relations, like wormholes or gravitational tunnels that serve as a "shortcut" through the—in this case—conceptual universe. I do count on the knowledge you as a reader have about superheroes to explain world issues. You will find yourself navigating easily between global dynamics and superhero narratives. However, I do not assume away any facts or details, both because scholarly knowledge should be laid out clearly . . . and because reviewing superhero biographies is fun!

Joseph Campbell discovered there was a universal common heroic narrative, which he called Monomyth or Hero's Journey. This structure or motif repeated across stories, cultures, and time, creating humanity´s common and shared experience. For Campbell, a heroic protagonist sets out, meets and overcomes a daunting set of challenges as a transformative adventure, and finally returns changed, empowered, and enlightened.[1] Present-day nation-states seem to be undergoing a similar symbolic path: (re)discovering the principles that make up national identity based on issues such as social integration, inequality, security, and immigration. At the same time, ethnic conflicts, humanitarian crises, massive human rights violations, and an impending planetary ecological catastrophe determine—consciously or not—a collective hero's journey for all mankind.

Why write a book on international relations with superheroes? Because it is fun. Isn't it frivolous, unserious? Not at all. The International Studies Association (ISA)—which brings together international studies at the global level—validated the pedagogical approach to explaining international studies through fiction in its journal *International Studies Perspectives*. I did not write this book as a fan of superheroes but as a PhD in international relations (a super-poor attempt at power). Here I introduce international studies with fun. I maintain rigor without losing recreation. I have done my investigation without forgetting my imagination. I write as an academic but without believing that academia should crush amazement, the astonishment we have when we are children and that made us see in a man who wears his underwear over his pants our greatest hero, that made us fancy when we went to the beach that we could telepathically communicate with dolphins, that drove us to stretch out our arm to see if we could sling spiderwebs.

The book is divided into four sections: main theories ("X-Ray Visions"), international structure ("The Multiverses"), issues in contemporary international relations ("Why We Fight"), and main actors on the world stage ("The Players"). Each chapter is informed by a superhero or supervillain. Some heroes and villains did not make it into this book. As in every good comic book story, they will most certainly appear in a sequel. I would gladly build this sequel from readers' comments and insights. For the time being, I hope that the emotional bond you have with superheroes and that most certainly led you to buy this book will take you back to your childhood so that you can go through these pages with the joy and enthusiasm with which they were written.

Acknowledgments

Thomas "Captain Canuck" Legler trusted me and this project from the beginning. Thank you for being a great colleague and an even greater friend.

Sergio "Charles Xavier" Berensztein has guided me in the development of my mutant skills for more than twenty years. Thank you for never giving up on me.

Eliot A. "Captain America" Cohen taught me courage and commitment should be one. Thank you, Sensei, for showing me study is service.

Part I

X-Ray Visions

International Relations Theories

The Talmud states we do not see things as they are but as we are. A theory is a set of propositions and concepts that combine to explain phenomena by specifying the relations among those propositions. Each theory indicates what part of reality we should observe: what data to record and what to discard. A theory establishes what causal connections we should establish between the data we collect and the phenomena we observe. Theories organize the information we observe. Based on this categorization, we create ideas about what the world is like. All theories contain a notion of human nature.

There are four main schools of thought in international studies: liberalism, realism, structuralism, and constructivism. All have made important contributions to the understanding of international politics, although they differ in what they are looking at. For each one, the world works according to different premises and precepts. None of the four is "better" than the other three. Otherwise, we would have only one of them in our toolkit. And none of them is totally useless; otherwise it would have already been discarded. Like Scott Summers needs his ruby-quartz lenses to control and direct his optic force blasts, theories act in the same way: they provide different vantage points from which to observe, explain, and predict world affairs.

Chapter One

Liberalism

The JLA

In 1941, the Justice Society of America (JSA) appeared in the third issue of *All Star Comics*. Writer Gardner Fox proposed to National Periodical Publications (later DC Comics) getting together all superheroes that did not reach the success of Batman or Superman. The founding members were the Atom, Doctor Fate, the Flash, Green Lantern, Hawkman, Hourman, Sandman, and the Spectre. These so-called mystery men were in fact superheroes acting as spies, protecting the home front of America during World War II. After American victory in the global confrontation, the JSA fell into oblivion. But in February 1960, *The Brave and the Bold* launched the Justice League of America (JLA): Batman, Superman, Wonder Woman, the Flash, Green Lantern, Aquaman, and the Martian Manhunter. The JLA was not the world's first superhero team. However, it is the standard by which all other superhero teams are measured.

Later, many other costumed heroes would appear in the JLA, including Hawkman and Hawkwoman, the Wonder Twins, Apache Chief, Green Arrow . . . and many more. This is the first aspect of liberalism the JLA illustrates: liberalism is a cosmopolitan political theory aimed at the entire global community of all humankind. Humans have inalienable rights, fundamental to every person. And there are thus universal rights, applicable to all peoples, in all states, religions, and cultures, without exception. In the same way, any superhero can be part of the JLA. Although it is true that the JLA is *American* by name, its members do not represent the interests of the United States. Liberals—in academia and in the JLA—advocate moral universalism: they claim liberal moral principles apply to all states. Even Superman renounces his American citizenship. In the nine hundredth edition of *Action*

Comics, Superman flies to Iran during a large protest. There he remains silent for a day, showing his support for the protesters amid expressions of appreciation (flowers and flags) and fear (Molotov cocktails).The government in Tehran sees Superman as an agent of the United States and understands his presence as an act of war. The Man of Steel reasons with cosmopolitan liberalism principles: "I am tired of my actions being interpreted as instruments of American policy." "Truth, justice, and the American way of life are no longer enough," he tells the US president's national security adviser. He then goes to the United Nations and relinquishes his citizenship.

Liberal theory has one application in international relations, but it goes far beyond this field of study. It is a philosophical tradition whose core is the belief that freedom is the foundation of human progress. For international relations liberalism, the concept of progress has a rational, a material, and a moral dimension directly related to the expansion of freedom. Liberalism holds human nature to be essentially good. Evil such as authoritarianism, injustice, and war is the by-product of foul human behavior or corrupt social institutions. Liberalism thus recovers the Greek idea that individuals are rational human beings, able to understand universally applicable laws governing both nature and human society. Understanding such laws means that people have the capacity to improve their condition by creating a more perfect society. Injustice, war, and aggression are not inevitable but can be moderated or even eliminated through institutional reform or collective action. Just as the Justice League has endured many roster changes to remain the earth's premier team of champions, so does international relations liberalism have different strands: political, economic, and institutional. The JLA illustrates the three kinds of answers liberalism has to offer for the central question of international relations: war and peace.

Political liberals argue that—over time—human beings tend toward increasingly free forms of exercising power. Following a historical evolution, rulers went from being incarnate gods to being envoys of the gods. They then were the fiercest warriors, the lords of the land, the sons of those landed chieftains . . . and finally, individuals who compete more or less fairly in an electoral arena. The JLA superheroes paradoxically combine the absolute power of antiquity with the accountability of modernity. The so-called interdemocratic peace explains war by the absence of structures of checks and balances. Politically more open regimes' politics imply more rationality in decisions and less violence in actions. Political liberals note more representative governments are built around higher degrees of freedom for individuals to decide for themselves. Liberal democratic republican regimes have a structure of conflict processing based on debate and dispute rather than coercion and combat. This facilitates dialogue and nonviolent resolution of disputes between citizens. At the international level, this also means they are less likely to fight each other because they have horizontal (different branches of government) and vertical (government-society) accountability. Republics have division of powers, and authority is based on laws (constitutions). The decision to go to war thus has to pass through several institutional instances. In democracies, there are frequent, free, transparent, and competitive elections. Rulers can be removed from office. Before deciding to go to war, a president considers his chances of reelection—something that absolute monarchs of antiquity or dictators are not subject to. More democratic regimes extend the prospects for peace in the world. The JLA does not aspire to become a praetorian guard for a universal cosmopolitan liberal political community. They are rather protectors of all world states, with the aspiration that they will develop internally just constitutions and become united in a confederation to ensure perpetual peace.

Economic liberalism stresses the uneconomical nature of war. Combat is a waste of resources for those involved, who may see their prosperity better served by trading rather than warfare. It is much better to be partners competing than enemies fighting. This liberal strand holds that when states are economically integrated (the operative term is *interdependent*), the incentives for armed confrontation diminish since in the event of war one would not be attacking an enemy but a supplier/buyer. Mutual ties reshape interests and interactions, favoring exchange over conquest. Within a global interdependent framework, military expansion implies closing off to peacetime business benefits: reduction in the availability of products, disruption of global value chains, increase in transport and energy costs, decrease in international investment. Moreover, for economic liberals, the advantages individual states gain from cooperation are irrelevant as long as there are absolute gains for all. Rather than focusing on who gains most, they focus on how to maximize gains for all participants. The same logic applies to membership and interaction between JLA members. Although there are more prominent figures (Batman, Superman), all JLA members bear equal responsibility and all benefit from collective action against evil. Today, interdependence is not only economic but also social and environmental. What happens in one part of the world has repercussions in another. These mutual effects prescribe a collective and cooperative approach to world affairs. Interdependence means that international relations are no longer a zero-sum game where what one party gains is necessarily the loss of another. These are precisely the kind of challenges the JLA faces. The JLA's ever-changing membership reflects the multiplicity and diversity of complex connections that create interdependencies between states and nonstate actors such as multinational companies and nongovernmental organizations. The talents of Superman and Batman are no longer enough by themselves.

Finally, liberal institutionalism believes global institutions allow resolution of collective action dilemmas in the international system. One problem of collective action is that everyone wants to enjoy a public good, but no one wants to pay the costs involved. (We will address international institutions specifically with Spider-Man.) Liberals support the effect international institutions have in shaping interests and behavior. As Robert Keohane (1988) defines, institutions are "persistent and connected sets of rules (formal and informal) that prescribe behavioral roles, constrain activity, and shape expectations." The United Nations (UN) helps less powerful states in the international system by providing them with an alternative way of advancing demands and resolving conflicts. The (liberal) superheroes of the JLA achieve the same objective with human beings: they pay the costs of planetary defense with their superpowers. The very idea of the JLA reflects what the field of international relations calls *multilateralism*. For realists, multilateralism is merely a means of strategic surveillance and balance between states. Any collective organization is for realists more similar to supervillain groupings, where characters bond not out of moral unity but coincident hatred of superheroes, or like the tortuous relations one can find between the characters of *Watchmen*. However, for liberalism, multilateralism implies an institutionalization process that cements belonging to an international community.

Separately, superheroes like Superman, Batman, Wonder Woman, the Flash, and Green Lantern are the greatest fighters for truth and justice the world has ever known. But collectively, they constitute an unstoppable material and moral force, a team of heroes who are only rivaled by the pantheons of gods from ancient mythology—the Justice League. The Hall of Justice is as close as one can get to the liberal faith in the potential of international institutions to deal with war, and the members of the JLA to the opportunity for collective problem solving in a multilateral forum. The JLA is what in international relations we call *collective security*; like Alexandre Dumas's characters D'Artagnan, Athos, Porthos, and Aramis, all superheroes who once passed through the JLA also share the dictum "all for one and one for all." Like super friends in the JLA, liberals aspire to Peace with a capital "P": not only the systematic absence of violence between states but a situation or condition in which war is no longer a material possibility. This aim runs straight from Immanuel Kant's "Perpetual Peace" to twentieth-century Wilsonianism. International liberalism was shaped by US President Woodrow Wilson, who authored the covenant of the League of Nations. This institution and its heir—the United Nations—share a basic proposition: war is preventable through collective security, whereby aggression by one state would be countered by automatic and collective reaction, embodied in a "league of nations." Collective security is more than adding power with circumstantial allies, such as the coalition that instrumentally united Churchill's English conservatism with Stalin's Soviet communism against Hitler's Nazism in World War II. Joint participation in an armed conflict is sustained by moral cohesion. This is why the JLA was also known as "Super Friends": it always has operational coordination because its members share collective principles.

Superheroes have no self-interest or individual interests that might collide with their joint action as members of the League. DC's official stance on the JLA is clear: "The League is the earth's first line of defense against threats too large for humanity to face alone. For decades, the Justice League has saved humanity from the worst threats it has ever faced." When the JLA uses force, it does so with aims and reach that go far beyond the territorial or strategic; their reach is humanitarian. When the JLA acts, Batman does not think about preserving Gotham, nor Superman Metropolis. Aquaman does not intervene in the world on behalf of the Atlanteans nor Diana Prince look after the interests of the Amazons. The JLA's (super)humanitarian interventions always have legitimacy because they are never confronted with the principle of territorial sovereignty of states or self-determination of peoples. The JLA serves the international community. The JLA's first enemy is an intergalactic star, Starro the Conqueror. The enemies of the JLA always want to destroy and dominate, so it seems a priori easy to agree that all their actions will be defensive, protective, and therefore fair. More recently, superheroes have strayed from the pristine exemplary model (*Hancock*, *Deadpool*, *Suicide Squad*) or been portrayed in a grim light that underlines their less than altruistic motives and personalities (*Watchmen*, *The Boys*). Such superheroes illustrate a modern-day conundrum for liberalism: what happens when power and principle do not coincide?

The enlightened imprint of liberalism understands that war is preventable and world peace achievable if religious, military, economic, or political restrictions and oppression are removed; that is, if the supervillains are defeated. For liberalism, war is an evil that can—and must—be prevented and eradicated. Conflict has an inherent moral component: there is an aggressor and a victim. The attacker is malicious, and the attacked is upright. All members of the international community or the JLA have a moral duty and material commitment to assist the victim and neutralize the aggressor. Liberals—like superheroes—believe in just war. There are moral justifications for war (human rights violations, crimes against humanity, genocide). At the same time, there is moral conduct in war (protection of civilians, humane treatment of the wounded or prisoners, and prohibition of torture). This Manichaeism is a methodological starting point for liberalism: republican and democratic regimes are open-minded in economic matters and active promoters of international multilateral institutions, while dictatorial or totalitarian regimes seek to close their borders to exchange (economic, political, cultural) while refusing to see their power limited by multilateral governance structures. Dividing the world into good and evil goes well beyond liberalism, and it is a staple of classic comic narratives: superheroes are good, beautiful, just, and noble; supervillains are bad, ugly, immoral, and vile. In Zack Snyder's *Man of Steel*, this stance is questioned when Superman kills General Zod. This was a radical change in the whole mythology of the Kryptonian, which prefigures the change of role of the United States in the world (as we see in detail in the chapter on hegemony). Was it legitimate to take his life? Is it a just response to the genocide Zod intended to carry out? What is the aim when using force? Is the destruction of the enemy necessary or is disarmament enough? Christopher Reeve's Superman would never have killed Zod. In the 1980 *Superman II* film by Richard Lester, the same conflict is resolved in a much more liberal way than in the 2013 remake.

Chapter Two

Batman's Realism

Political realism is the product of a long historical and philosophical tradition to studying politics in general and international politics in particular. It is perhaps the oldest and most influential tradition. Little Bruce Wayne has all the makings of a perfect realist. The fate that led him to become the Dark Knight made him embody the first lesson of realism: human nature does not change. Human beings must be taken as they really are (hence *realism*, in opposition to liberalism's optimistic stance) rather than in an ideal condition or gradual evolution. Besides being invariable, human nature is quite infamous as well: humans are selfish, self-interested, and constantly seeking power. The result is a state of nature, a state of war of all against all, actual or potential, mistrust, permanent competition, and continuous fear. The line between objectivist and fatalist becomes blurred since realism also postulates that the human condition has not changed and will not change. As such, the lessons from Greek historian Thucydides, Florentine political scientist Nicholas Machiavelli, Chinese strategist Sun Tzu, or English philosopher Thomas Hobbes remain constant and valid as the iron laws of international politics.

From this pessimistic starting point on human nature, realism develops a tragic conception of international politics: the competition for power is unending and unceasing and the threat of hostilities between states perpetual. The world is not an opportunity but a peril. There are many branches within realism, but they all see states as the central actors in world affairs. States are by definition the legitimate and territorial monopoly of force and therefore the fundamental actors in international relations. They also share a focus on power and security. States act as individuals, in a unitary way in pursuit of their own survival. The individual fights for self-preservation in the state of nature in the same way states interact in the international system. Survival is guaranteed through the attainment of security. States must provide security for themselves, as no other agency or actor can be counted on to do so.

When Thomas Hobbes describes human existence as "solitary, poore, nasty, brutish, and short," he could have been describing the fateful alley that orphaned Gotham's heir. Wayne Junior understood that the world is hostile and that to survive in it one must accumulate power. Security is only possible by increasing power. Power, in turn, is thought by realists in terms of the material resources necessary to physically coerce other states: the capacity to fight and win wars. In the realist logic, states seek power to survive conflict and procure their own security. Anarchy in international relations is not chaos but the absence of hierarchy in the system. In the (anarchic) world of Batman, there is no central authority with the capacity and will to impose on the rest. Since there is no world government—there is no "global 911"—conflict is permanent. And it will never be resolved since there is no state on the global stage capable of imposing its victory in the way a nation-state does on the domestic level. The closest thing to that would be . . . Superman (we will address that in the chapter on world order). Just as the police and the courts could not help Bruce in preventing the bullets that killed Thomas and Martha Wayne, realists cannot rely on international laws, codes, agreements, regimes, or institutions. Neither international law nor multilateral organizations can provide credible deterrence. In the film *Batman vs. Superman*, Zack Snyder chooses to tell the story of the fateful night depicting Thomas Wayne (Bruce's father) fighting the criminal Joe Chill rather than meekly attempting to placate him as was the classic Batman narrative tradition. For realism, the greater the force, the lesser the number of enemies and threats and so the lower the risk of being destroyed. Acquiescence and appeasement are responses to the strength of others that stem from weakness. Batman seems to have followed the advice of the Roman military historian Vegetius: "He who desires peace must prepare for war." Like a nation-state, Bruce *became* Batman; he dedicated his life to becoming strong and overcoming weakness. Realists are skeptical that trade, democracy, international institutions, or scientific progress can lead to peace. Batman's actions are not like the JLA's liberalism: the Dark Knight is closer to human revenge than Olympic justice.

International politics is to realism a succession of balances of power between the most powerful, in which the weak states have few options: follow the leader or suffer the consequences. Thucydides described the Athenians threatening the Melians during the Peloponnesian war: "As things happen in the world, the strong impose their power when they can; it is up to the weak to suffer what they must; a necessary law." Realism's notion of power is like Batman's: conceived essentially in military terms. The distribution of power between states determines their conduct in the system. Realism understands that states are guided by a clear and unchanging national interest and anything unrelated to that—such as trade or finance, gender equality, or the environment—necessarily takes a back seat in terms of foreign policy priority. Economic activity is a means for augmenting state security. This is also the realist view on international institutions: international organizations do not alter the behavior of the state because they only exist through power. They reflect and reinforce the existing distribution of power. States create international law and institutions to enforce codified rules that serve their own interests and perpetuate power relations. States will always act to protect their own objectives guided by national interest defined in terms of power. International action must for realists therefore be based on a dispassionate analysis of circumstances rather than on philosophical principles or moral values. It must be a policy of reality, based on concrete interests and willing to do what is necessary. War, espionage, secrecy, and violence are indispensable instruments of international policy. For Carl von Clausewitz (1976), war was "the continuation of politics by other means." The same could be said of realist foreign policy as Commissioner Jim Gordon says of Batman: "He's the hero Gotham deserves, but not the one it needs right now. So we'll hunt him. Because he can take it. Because he's not our hero. He's a silent guardian. A watchful protector. A Dark Knight."

There are objective rules and patterns of interaction to world affairs. The most important one for realism is that the essence of international interaction is the struggle for power. There cannot be a power capable of dominating and thus putting an end to this endless competition. Hence, international relations are a constant game of security alliances, power balances, or deterrence. Realists assume unitary, homogeneous, coherent, and rational states with perfect information and full knowledge of their own interests based on a perfect judgment of their relative position of power vis-à-vis their (actual or potential) enemies. In the *balance of power*, the different actors in the system seek to balance each other out by trying to prevent anyone from having the power to impose itself over the rest. The sum of small powers can balance out the disparity with the greater one. Multiple, crossed, flexible, and secret alliances are generated with the aim of achieving balance and preventing domination. Alliances do not imply moral unity like we have seen with the JLA. In fact, "United Nations" is the name of the alliance formed by Stalin's Soviet communism, Churchill's English conservatism, and Roosevelt's American democratic progressivism. Alliances resemble those comics episodes in which superheroes and villains are circumstantially and pragmatically brought together. *Deterrence* entails amassing power in such a differential degree that it will discourage any enemy by means of understanding the futility of aggression through the certainty of his own destruction: deterrence by intimidation or retaliation. This deterrent principle clearly does not work in the superhero universe: if it did, there would be no confrontation and every supervillain would know in advance that—because of an insurmountable power differential—the contest against superheroes is pointless. An economically and physically fragile individual with schizotypal personality disorder like Arthur Fleck should know *ex ante* that he does not stand a chance against the richest man in Gotham, trained and assisted by a technological arsenal. Nonetheless, he puts up quite a fight. The same example could apply to the Malvinas/Falklands campaign of the Argentine government against the United Kingdom in 1982, the 2001 Al-Qaeda attacks against the United States, or the 2021 Hamas rockets against Israel. Deterrence assumes the attacker (a) to be rational and (b) to value his own existence more than the disappearance of his enemy's. What can be done then to frighten those who are not afraid to die? As Alfred rightly reminds Bruce: "Some men aren't looking for anything logical, like money. They can't be bought, bullied, reasoned, or negotiated with. Some men just want to watch the world burn."

Chapter Three

Constructivism

Between Harvey Dent and Two-Face

Constructivism is an ontology that questions the dominant way of thinking about international politics, in particular, the rationalist and positivist claim of objectivity from the liberal and realist theories. International relations do not exist solely "out there." Constructivists reject the idea that truth can simply be "read" into objects. Kant himself had already shown that causality was not a property of the world but of human reason. Since the world is historically determined and socially constructed, knowledge cannot be confined to material reality. It must include ideas and identities as well as interests. Hence, constructivists focus their analysis on the meanings ascribed by the subjects to objects. As a theory of international politics, constructivism emphasizes the social construction of the world in opposition to a materialistic and objectivist vision such as liberalism (based on interests) or realism (centered on power and security). Neither objects nor concepts have a necessary, fixed, or objective meaning. Meanings are constructed through social interaction. World politics appears to constructivism as intersubjective: it derives from the decisions, perceptions, and relations between subjects rather than from essential objective characteristics. State behavior is shaped by elite beliefs, identities, and social norms. Individuals and collectivities forge, shape, and change culture through ideas and practices.

Harvey Dent was Gotham City's gentle and courteous district attorney. An ally of Batman, he fought to make the city a better place and reform its criminals. However, his life got out of control after Sal "Boss" Maroni threw sulfuric acid in his face during a trial and disfigured the left side. Dent had concealed from the public a bipolarism, and this trauma aggravated Dent's condition. By releasing his hidden dark side, Dent becomes Two-Face, the disturbed embodiment of the prosecutor's inner demons. A dual nature understanding of reality is made visible by Dent's external appearance: a divided face. Sometimes Dent's good side wins. Other times, the evil Two-Face prevails. Harvey Dent is a man of the law; Two-Face is a criminal hell-bent on taking over Gotham. Both sides come together to create a multifaceted villain in the same way the objective and intersubjective come together in constructivism's understanding of a multifaceted international reality. Like liberals and realists, constructivists see power as important. However, where the former see power in primarily material terms (military, economic, political), constructivists also see power in discursive terms (ideas, culture, and language).

Alexander Wendt gives an excellent example that illustrates the social construction of reality when he explains that five hundred British nuclear weapons are less threatening to the United States than five North Korean ones. This is not because of the number of atomic bombs (material structure) but because of the meaning in which such possession occurs (the structure of ideas, which states London is friend and Pyongyang, enemy). State and national interests are the result of the social identities of actors. It is not the distribution of material capabilities but the set of converging or diverging meanings and identities that will determine how the distribution of capabilities is interpreted and, consequently, national interest and the ways in which states are going to pursue or protect it. Dent shares with Wendt the centrality of identities, representations of the state's understanding of itself, of others, and of the international system. Identities are socially constructed through interaction. Intersubjectivity shapes the perception of states' own interests and defines the set of behavior preferences or prescriptions. This will in turn determine the range of possible actions. Dent resolves this dilemma by letting the infamous coin toss decide his actions. If it lands on the unscarred side, Dent commits a benevolent act. If the coin lands on the scarred side, then Two-Face takes over and follows through with crime and murder. In the natural world, one can infer reaction from action. For example, if I kick a ball, I can anticipate—by the force and direction of my kick, accounting for my internal bias and external factors such as wind—its trajectory and final position. But in the social world, if I kick a sleeping dog, it can go back to sleep, move, go away, start playing, or launch an attack depending on the subjective relation between the dog and me. Two-Face understands well the gap constructivism highlights between objectivity and subjectivity, rules and behavior, when he reproaches Batman in the film *The Dark Knight Rises*: "You thought we could be decent men in an indecent time. But you were wrong. The world is cruel, and the only morality in a cruel world is chance. Unbiased. Unprejudiced. Fair."

Constructivists ascribe a central role to social norms in international politics. Jepperson, Wendt, and Katzenstein (1996, 34) define them as "standards of behavior appropriate to actors with a given identity." Norms become expected conduct when a critical mass of relevant state actors adopt them and internalize them into their identity. States that conform to a given identity are expected to act according to the standards associated with that identity. The split between the Dent and Two-Face personalities represents the centrality of norms. Structure (the shape of the international system) and agency (the ability to act) are mutually constituted, as are both parts of Dent's face. Following Wildavsky (1994), there are no interests without subjects. And international subjects are embedded in cultures that create normative structures within which those interests are generated. Thus, interests and identities are for constructivism a highly malleable result of specific historical processes. For example, Australia supported the 2003 Iraq War, while Canada did not. Based on different domestic cultures, Canadian and Australian leaders made different choices. Ottawa was immersed in a normative framework of peaceful conflict resolution through negotiation and multilateral institutions. Canberra focused on complying with partnership obligations and commitments within a mutual defense framework. Structures limit the agency of states, and agency can change structures. Indeed, world politics is always under construction and change. Instead of taking the state for granted and assuming that it simply seeks survival or wealth, constructivists posit states act in accordance to their identity and that it is possible to predict when this identity manifests itself as a causal variable explaining international relations. International relations of enmity or friendship are not preordained or fatally determined by external variables. The dynamic, intersubjective structure of shared ideas and beliefs can transform or reinforce the existing patterns of cooperation or conflict. As meanings are not fixed, they can change over time depending on the ideas and beliefs of the actors. Change can occur within a national setting and cross-nationally through socialization, diffusion of ideas, and internationalization of norms. When a state's identity changes, constructivists investigate the effect that this change in identity has on the state's behaviors. They inquire about the process of (re)construction of identity in order to discover the discursive elements that transform social reality. A constructivist perspective would argue that most states have joined together to develop climate change mitigation policies because it is the right thing to do for the survival of humanity. After decades of diplomacy, it has become an appropriate behavior that most citizens expect their leaders to adhere to. In Frank Miller's *Batman: The Dark Knight Returns*, Two-Face is given a chance at redemption with plastic surgery to rebuild the disfigured half of his face and psychiatric treatment. Batman realizes Harvey Dent sees himself with both sides of his face scarred. In a constructivist dialogue, Batman argues he is "not fooled by vision; I see him as he is." Although at first the Bat hero believes Dent to have recovered, Two-Face takes the city hostage with a bomb. It becomes clear that the villainous identity is in permanent

control. Dent looks at his face and says, "At least now both sides are even"—
the final socialization of the pair, constructivism at its best.

Chapter Four

Red Son and Structuralism

Structuralism—as an analytical perspective rather than a political doctrine—believes that in order to understand human society, it is necessary to understand the nature of material production and exchange. Karl Marx—from whom the structuralist perspective derives—sought to understand alienation, a distinct type of social ill whose diagnosis looks to rest on his controversial account of human nature and its bourgeoning. Material life determines social life. Thus, the primary direction of social explanation is from material production to social forms and thence to forms of consciousness. Marx developed a theory of history—historical materialism—centered around the idea that forms of society rise and fall as they advance and later constrain the development of human productive power. Historical materialism asserts that human beings, including the relations between them and their environment, are determined by material conditions. As the material means of production develop, economic structures rise and fall. *Factors* of production (capital, labor, land, and technology) have been combined in different ways throughout history to give rise to different *modes* of production: slavery, feudalism, communism, and capitalism. Marx studied closely the contemporary capitalist mode of production and found it to be driven by a remorseless pursuit of profit, whose origins are found in the extraction of surplus value from the "exploited proletariat." Capitalism's dirty secret is that it is not a realm of harmony and mutual benefit but a system in which one class prevails through systematic profit extraction. The rich get richer and the poor get poorer.

Markets produce a "laissez unfair" state of affairs. In a constant struggle, social classes that possess the *means* of production—wealth and the way of creating it—will try to preserve this privilege by creating ruling structures. *Relations* of production are the political and institutional frameworks that regulate ownership to safeguard control of productive resources and thus protect the position of the dominant classes. Structuralism does not focus its concern on power but on domination. And that domination is economic.

Red Son is Mark Millar's imagining of what would have happened if Superman had been brought up in the Soviet Union. Millar intersperses alternative versions of superheroes from DC Comics with alternative-reality versions of real political figures like Joseph Stalin and John F. Kennedy. Superman's capsule lands in a Ukrainian *kolkhoz* (collective farm) instead of on the property of *farmer* Jonathan Kent in Kansas. As a result, instead of fighting for "truth, justice, and the American way," Superman ends up being a "champion of the common worker who fights a never-ending battle for Stalin, socialism, and the international expansion of the Warsaw Pact." Unlike realism and liberalism, Marxism rejects the autonomy of politics and maintains instead that economic factors determine international phenomena and the state and politics are *epiphenomena*. Marx and Engels call the economic structure of a society an *infrastructure* or *base* and the legal and political institutions (the nation-state, the law, and the ideology that supports domination) *superstructures. Red Son* is Superman without the superstructure of American liberal democracy.

The modern world order is not the result of a certain distribution of power or the presence of international institutions but the product of the expansion of global capitalism. International relations are about the relations among the means of production, social relations, and power. Uneven global economic development patterns empower and enslave different social classes and thus states and corporations. An "instrumental" model portrays the state as simply a tool, directly controlled by the economically dominant class to further its own interests at the expense of the interests both of other classes and of the community as a whole. This can be particularly relevant in today's world when analyzing issues concerning climate change and the ecology-economy dilemma. Second, the "class balance" model portrays the state as having interests of its own, with capitalist interests as merely one of them in the midst of warring classes of contemporary society. Capitalist interests are a political constraint on state action rather than its primary goal. A final "abdication" model presents the bourgeoisie as staying away from the direct exercise of political power but doing this because it is in their economic interests to do so.

This perspective links geopolitical changes to capitalist crises: the structure of the international system is the result of the expansion of capitalism by means of imperialism. British economist John A. Hobson theorized that expansion occurs because of three conditions in developed states: overproduction of goods and services, underconsumption by workers and lower classes (due to low wages), and oversaving from upper classes and the bourgeoisie. To overcome this hindering to wealth production, developed states have historically expanded abroad: goods thus find new markets in underdeveloped regions, workers' wages are kept low because of foreign competition, and savings are profitably invested in new markets. The world capitalist system is characterized by an unequal division of labor between the periphery and the center. This critical characteristic generates and perpetuates an ever-widening economic gap between the rich core and the poor periphery. Politically, it gives rise to a relation of domination and dependence from which the "underdeveloped" (currently more politely dubbed "developing" or "emerging") countries cannot escape. For structuralists, imperialism generates a hierarchical international system. Developed countries can expand, enabling them to sell goods and export surplus wealth that they cannot use at home. Developing countries are increasingly constrained by and dependent on advanced countries. Through colonialism first and economic dependence later (through international trade and indebtedness), the central/advanced countries dominate the peripheral/emerging ones. Emerging or developing countries are economically exploited and weakened by transnational capital: advanced states and multinational corporations in complicity with international organizations and with the consent of local elites on the periphery. Imperialism leads, however, to rivalry among developed countries. Where economic liberals maintain equilibrium will be found through the market, structuralists critique capitalism as inevitably leading to crises. In the twenty-first century, global capitalism reproduces itself in a coercive and consensual way. Neo-Gramscian radical perspectives focus on the domination through consensual methods. International organizations and laws reproduce capitalism and its inequalities. Structural power—the power to decide how things shall be done, to shape frameworks within which states relate to each other, to people, or to corporations—is not a national attribute born out of political superiority but the consequence of control over economic resources. A transnational capitalist "superclass" forms a "global civil society" that universalizes liberal ideals instead of imposing itself through more coercive processes of classical imperialism and colonization. As a theory of economic determinism, structuralism helps us understand the role of economic forces, both within and between states. It is also a viewpoint advocating major change in the international system through its critical stance toward issues such as income inequality and social exclusion.

The history of the Soviet Superman follows a structure consistent with the theoretical prescriptions of structuralism. The radical/Marxian tradition sees historical analysis as revealing necessary outcomes. A "vanguard" Superman remains noble, just, and dedicated to the cause of communism. A child orphaned in a political purge becomes a Batman who is also Soviet. However, instead of a billionaire, he is the leader of an anarchist terrorist organization. And Wonder Woman is an ambassador following the Marxist postulate that the fundamental actors in international relations are not states but social classes. On the US side, Lex Luthor seems to represent both capitalist ingenuity and the excesses and abuses of individual freedom. Neither *Red Son*'s narrative nor the structure of the Marxist theoretical model focus on the issues of war and peace. They direct attention to economic structure, inequality, poverty, and exploitation within and between nations. When the suspicious head of the People's Commissariat of Internal Affairs, Pyotr Roslov, poisons Stalin, Superman initially declines the leadership of the party. It is only when he meets up again with his former childhood friend Lana Lazarenko and sees her suffering and that of her children that Superman realizes that his powers could be used for greater good. The soviet superhero abandons his "false consciousness." The *tovarich* Superman becomes class conscious and takes the leadership of the country in order to advance socialism to a global utopia. Disciplined and organized as Marxism prescribes, Soviet Superman reins in the revolutionary energies of the masses that would otherwise remain dispersed and unconcentrated under a provisional state apparatus to facilitate the inevitable transition to communism through an intermediary stage, a "dictatorship of the proletariat." Between 1950—when *Red Son* was initiated—and 2001, Luthor's United States confronts Superman's USSR (as the CIA did during the Cold War): he builds a clone of Superman (Bizarro), which is sacrificed to save millions after provoking an accidental nuclear missile launch in Great Britain. Luthor attempts to reduce Moscow but fails when his collaborator Brainiac miniaturizes Stalingrad. Then Luthor seeks regime change via destabilization by encouraging the anarchist Batman terrorist network, which sees the abundance that Superman's system imposes on people as little more than oppression. Wonder Woman has fallen in love with Superman, but he sees her simply as a comrade. By 2001 the Global Soviet Union encompasses all countries except Chile and the divided remnants of the United States, which suffered a disastrous civil war in 1986 in which sixteen unidentified states broke away from the union. The Superman-led USSR has grown without resorting to war and has no crime, poverty, disease, or unemployment. Superman becomes the dictator of the proletariat on the road to communism. Because of his superpowerful condition, Red Kal-El can embody this historical process, the perfect illustration of Marx's *dictum*: "Communism is the riddle of history solved, and it knows itself to be this solution." He is a fantasy leader of parties that countries as diverse as the Soviet Union, China, Cuba, and North Korea have adopted, with disastrous humanitarian results.

Chapter Five

Dr. Strange's Intersectional Perspective

Vain and egotistic surgeon Dr. Stephen Strange loses the use of his hands in a car crash caused by his own recklessness. Having lost soon after his fortune in a series of costly, complicated, and experimental surgeries, he seeks a cure far off the beaten path of modern medicine. In Nepal, Strange is saved by Mordo, a disciple of the Ancient One, who, as Earth's Sorcerer Supreme, holds many mysteries of the Old World. The Ancient One refuses to guide Strange through the process until he relinquishes his selfishness and opens his mind to a higher truth. This higher truth is a different understanding of power, what feminist perspectives hold as their key contribution: exposing and deconstructing socially constructed gendered power. Identities are socially constructed expectations and normative ideas attached to men and women. Feminist scholars use gender analysis to deconstruct the theoretical frameworks behind international relations, interrogating gender bias embedded in core concepts and concerns such as states, sovereignty, power, security, international conflict, and global governance. Poststructuralism further redefines the scope and bounds of the political and even the very concept of power. Inspired by Michel Foucault, power is viewed as a mobile and constantly shifting set of force relations that emerge from every social interaction. International relations no longer focus exclusively on states as the sole concentrations of power in the system, opening up analysis to how power flows through the capillaries of the global body politic. Foucault does not deny the repressive function of power. He rejects the one-dimensionality of assuming power is fundamentally repressive. Power simultaneously creates subjects and subjects them: "The individual is not the vis-à-vis of power; it is, I believe, one of its prime effects" (1980, 98). Foucault maintains power produces reality: "It produces domains of objects and rituals of truth" (1977,

21

194). The Ancient One would agree: power is "the source code that shapes reality."

During his training, Stephen learns about the Multiverse and the ancient science of magic, as well as forbidden knowledge. Intersectionality in international relations means opening up an analytic Multiverse, understanding that world affairs are shaped not only by gender but also by other identities, such as race, ethnicity, nationality, and class. By "intersections," feminists refer to the interconnectedness of gendered identities, structures of domination, discrimination, oppression, exploitation, and violence. Intersectionality refers to where these identities intersect and in turn how different groups of people are marginalized from mainstream views. Intersectional analysis constitutes a paradigm shift away from the monolithic representation of gender relations as the patriarchal domination of women by men without regard to race, ethnicity, and sexual and colonial hierarchies. It thus no longer refers only to the singular axis of difference between women and men. It opens up multiple axes of difference so that we take account of poor, minority, migrant, and refugee women and girls who have often fallen through the categories of feminist and international relations theories, global policy, and international law. In addition to his ability to teleport across a single plane, the mystical warrior showcases the ability to travel between dimensional planes and access alternate dimensions. Like Strange, intersectionality stands on multiple vantage points to analyze international relations. Like the fragmented, psychedelic, shape-centric, kaleidoscopic "form constant" visuals that appear all through the film version, international *relations* are the sum of all international *realities.*

In time, Strange becomes adept at astral projection, sending his astral self away from his body and allowing him to observe events without the knowledge of those present. This is akin to intersectional perspectives' moral and ontological self-reflexivity about potential exclusions. Intersectionality means being conscious of the political exclusions that result from normative purposes and from the choices of research subject and methodology and taking responsibility for these exclusions, something the self-centered surgeon does not understand. In Scott Derrickson's 2016 *Doctor Strange*, when Strange first walks into Kamar-Taj, he assumes Master Hamir to be the Ancient One just because he is a man. Intersectional perspectives require sensitivity to power in all places within and beyond the conventional or conceptual boundaries of states and international public spheres. This leads them to ask questions not only about the powerful but also about their relationship to the powerless.

Strange: Really? Are you sure you got the right place? That one looks a little more . . . Kamar-Taj-y.

Mordo: I once stood in your place. And I, too, was . . . disrespectful. So might I offer you some advice. Forget everything you think you know.

Not by chance is this knowledge deep in fictional Kamar-Taj in Nepal. Dr. Strange's narrative follows another to intersectional perspectives. Postcolonial theory emphasizes the contemporary world cannot be understood without taking into account colonial history and the domination of the West over the rest of the world for several centuries. Latin American, Asian, and African countries have been politically decolonized, but invisible mechanisms of domination have not ended. Discourses reaffirm unequal relations through representation of a nondemocratic and nonrational "uncivilized other." Known as "othering," this process refers to how groups of people attribute negative characteristics to other individuals or groups of people that set them apart as representing that which is opposite to the original group. Colonial normative discourses constituted what is possible, natural, or correct and what constituted legitimate knowledge and thus whose voices were heard. International relations are themselves practices of production of *otherness*, practices of domination over others to justify a certain international social and political order. Postcolonial theory incorporates the voice of marginalized individuals and traditionally silenced groups. When Strange and Mordo stroll toward Kamar-Taj, they walk by a group of Sadhu holy men. Mordo keeps going and stops in front a wooden door (coincidentally or not, this six-panel door is known as a *colonial* door).

Strange enters Kamar-Taj a doctor. In his work on medicine, Foucault revealed how values have been built into the epistemological framework underlying modern medicine. What is regarded as "normal" often conflates usual or typical with what ought to be. Consequently, there can be no purely scientific or objective definition of "the normal" in medicine. Health cannot even be defined as normality either. Feminist perspectives challenge international relations' "normality" just as Kamar-Taj challenges Strange's Western medicine normality:

The Ancient One: You're a man who's looking at the world through a keyhole, and you spent your whole life trying to widen that keyhole. To see more, know more. And now, on hearing that it can be widened in ways you can't imagine, you reject the possibility?

Dr. Stephen Strange: No, I reject it because I do not believe in fairy tales about chakras or energy or the power of belief. There is no such thing as spirit! We are made of matter and nothing more. We're just another tiny, momentary speck within an indifferent universe.

The Ancient One: You think you know how the world works? You think that this material universe is all there is? What is real? What mysteries lie beyond the reach of your senses? At the root of existence, mind and matter meet. Thoughts shape reality. This universe is only one of an infinite number.

Narrative-based, interpretive, and ethnographic international relations capture the social, constitutive aspects of world politics in ways rationalist, dominant Western perspectives cannot. *Doctor* Stephen Strange leaves Kamar-Taj *Master* Strange.

Part II

The Multiverses

Global Structure

In this section, we address four characteristics that shape our world: world order, globalization, the consolidation of digital technologies, and the diffusion of international institutions. The four of them provide the background to a multifaceted, multidimensional understanding of international relations.

Acoustics of the performance venue have an impact on a singer's performance. Even if artists are unaware, their repertoire is sensitive and vulnerable to changes in the acoustic environment. In the same way, the final outcome of international actions, processes, and strategies is contingent upon and dependent on the global structure. The four interdependent traits taken together combine to provide the stage on which global interactions occur.

Chapter Six

Superman

Hegemony and World Order

According to realism, the structure of the international system is determined by the distribution of power among states. There are three possible distributions: multipolar (more than two states competing for power and influence), bipolar (two contenders compete to extend their influence to the rest of the world), or unipolar (when a hegemonic state concentrates economic and military power in a dominant manner in the system). Power constitutes the essential underpinning of world order, which is itself the structure within which international interactions take place. Order has then an authoritative component; it flows from top to bottom in a more or less consensual, hierarchical, or imperial structure. The term *hegemony* comes from the Greek word *hēgemonía*, which means supremacy. Applied to current world affairs, it means leadership exercised by a single state. A global hegemon requires an extraordinary material capacity plus a set of political, economic, social, and cultural ideas to attract followers to the system it proposes/imposes. In the most basic sense, an international order is an established pattern of relations and behavior between the actors of a system. Order simply describes a relation between elements in a system based on some principle (power). It does not imply intentionality, coherence, or values such as stability, prosperity, or peace. One of the most fundamental concerns in international relations is how order is established, maintained, and destroyed.

There has probably never been a truly global world order. What we call an *order* was devised in Western Europe almost four centuries ago at a peace conference in the German region of Westphalia after a century of sectarian conflict and political turmoil across the continent, ending in the Thirty Years' War (1618–1648). To put an end to a series of political and religious conflicts that claimed almost a quarter of Europe's population, a set of arrangements was defined that survives to this day. The system was built around independent states that have internal sovereignty (the maximum authority within the territory is the state) and external equality (agreement not to interfere in the internal affairs of others). The so-called Peace of Westphalia recognized a practical reality: a multiplicity of autonomous political units, internally diverse and externally not powerful enough to defeat all others. This would guarantee the general balance of power and stability without resorting to any divine dimension or the claim of universal government. Order born out of multiplicity and moderation, diversity and division. However, the European-born organizational structure claimed universal validity. Throughout history, all regions have believed governing their own areas of influence to be equivalent to ordering the whole world. Perceiving their own order as unique leads to dismissing other parts of the world as strange or "barbaric." The so-called *Pax Romana* and *Pax Britannica* created an international order of relative peace and security that guaranteed the international expansion of economic profit and political power.

During the twentieth century, it would be the United States' turn to become the indispensable defender of what it termed the international liberal order. However, the *Pax Americana* was not based on the European balance of power but on achieving peace through the spread of economic (market) and political (democracy) freedom. In the Second World War, Washington defeated Nazism and then created the North Atlantic Treaty Organization (NATO) to contain the advance of Soviet totalitarianism. It helped rebuild the devastated European economies and formed a global multilateral network of economic, political, and security institutions. The American-led order had the idealism and material resources to take on the task of building an order that would overcome the economic recession of the 1930s and ensure that victory achieved in 1945 would prevent a third world war. Although selective and conditioned by the national security needs of the Cold War, this order supported participatory governance in the countries under its aegis to a degree never seen before in the history of world hegemons. The United States emerged from the Cold War as the world's only superpower with the mission to sustain and extend its power across the globe. All the postwar presidents up to Donald Trump ratified the exceptional role of the United States in the world (Superman's Kryptonian father famously tells him: "Even though you've been raised as a human being, you are not one for them"), convinced of the indispensability of American power. Moral universalism underpinned US foreign policy based on the belief in freedom—political and economic—as the fundamental pillar for the organization of human life. Like the United States, Superman conceives his superpowers not as a retaliatory instrument to punish villains but as a capacity to improve the lives of all men. Victory is understood not as support for domination but as a means of expanding freedom. The applicability of American principles to the world was adopted as a dogma: "World peace cannot be established without the United States," Woodrow Wilson established in 1919. And president George W. Bush would ratify this eighty-four years later in a different way: "The liberty we prize is not our gift to the world; it is God's gift to humanity."

A slightly more critical perspective on American hegemony—and on Superman himself—is seen in the film *Batman v. Superman*. In Frank Miller's original comics, the American president sends Superman to stop Batman after he assassinates the Joker. But in the film, Batman tries to end the hegemony of the Kryptonian after having seen the pitched battle between Superman and Zod in which Metropolis is half obliterated and human lives are taken. Is it this unstoppable destruction that gets Batman thinking about the dangers of having a superhero with god-like powers? Bruce Wayne understands the danger of Superman's hegemony: "If he wanted to, he could burn the whole place down and there wouldn't be a damn thing we could do to stop him," he snaps out in a conversation with Clark Kent. Wayne has a Gramscian view of Superman's hegemony: the consensual or legitimizing element underpins dominance by giving it a cultural dimension beyond coercion. Lois Lane's praise of Superman's exploits in the *Daily Planet* is what Gitlin (1979) calls "prime time ideology": the hegemonic process imposed through journalistic narrative.

Superman expresses and embodies the idea of a liberal order in a superheroic manner. It is power and principle, capacity and will, invulnerability and incorruptibility. He obeys laws and respects presidents, but he is not afraid to go against wickedness and malice to help people. He fights the archetype of the corrupt billionaire with pretensions to privilege (Lex Luthor; see the chapter on inequality) and always sides with the common man: miners, farmers, minorities, and anyone who needs a hand. His view seems to be taken from President John F. Kennedy's inaugural speech in 1961, when he said that the United States would "pay any price, bear any burden, face any difficulty, support any friend, and oppose any enemy to ensure the survival and success of freedom." Superman gave up his citizenship and even his own life for the greater good. This "big blue Boy Scout" from Kansas is America at it its best. The adopted son of farmers in the country's farm belt, Clark learns the values that are the backbone of American self-perception. In the eighteenth century, William Penn described the United States as "the country of a poor and good man," emphasizing notions of egalitarianism, just governance, and moderation in economic pursuits. Benjamin Franklin described the American as "austere, industrious, and frugal." And Seymour Martin Lipset termed "American exceptionalism" the nation's ideology. This he described in five words: liberty, egalitarianism, individualism, populism, and laissez-faire. Superman takes the American dream to a planetary scale in the same way that the United States builds international order by projecting its own internal characteristics on the global stage. Only Superman could do this: while in comics Wonder Woman appears as a Republican and Batman as a Democrat, the Kryptonian is always above party affiliations. Superman is a superhero for humankind as American hegemony is a "beacon of freedom" for the world—a "shining city upon a hill": a proud, God-blessed example for humanity, teeming with people of all kinds living in harmony and peace and humming with commerce and creativity. In addition to projecting power, both promise hope. Superman's biological father, Jor-El, tells his son something akin to the creed of American hegemony: "Live as one of them, Kal-El, to discover where your strength and your power are needed. But always hold in your heart the pride of your special heritage. They can be a great people, Kal-El; they wish to be. They only lack the light to show the way. For this reason above all, their capacity for good, I have sent them you, my only son."

Chapter Seven

The Flash as Globalization

The Flash is "the fastest man alive." He fights evil using his extraordinary speed, derived from a mysterious power known as the Speed Force, an energy field that grants incredible powers of velocity. Three generations have worn the crimson speedster suit: Jay Garrick, Barry Allen, and Wally West. Jay Garrick fell asleep in a laboratory and inhaled the fumes produced by his experiment. Waking up with superhuman speed, he decided to become a superhero. Barry Allen was a police chemist also working in his lab one night when lightning struck a shelf of chemicals. Wally West was in his uncle Barry's lab when he was in the same accident that transformed Barry. Wally took up the mantle at a time when Barry was considered dead. But when Barry returned, he became the Flash once again. Like globalization, the Flash extolls the power of science and technology—and not in an admonishing way of warning about its dangers as is the case with the Hulk, Dr. Manhattan, or Dr. Doom. For these characters, the terrifying and dangerous side of uncontrolled science is manifested. The Flash shares with globalization this faith in technological utopia, the hope of constant technical progress: always on the move, moving forward, improving. The Flash is globalized progress personified.

The multiple incarnations of the Flash help us understand the first fundamental aspect of this term widely used and much more widely abused. What is globalization? Globalization is the most salient structural feature of today's world system. It is the setting in which all international events take place, existing through multiple dimensions: physical (environment, natural resources, climate), social (technology, economy, and society), political (local, national, and global governance), cultural (language, food, art), and spiritual (religion, identity). Globalization is also the result of many concurrent and contradictory causes. The Flash is typically drawn with motion lines extending behind his body to indicate his path and speed. This "stroboscopic technique" (called "blurgits") creates the visual experience of seeing an object (or subject in this case) in super-speed motion. Similarly, the multiplicity of levels of analysis and explanatory variables make precisely pinning down globalization very difficult. I propose a definition of globalization to help us make sense of the fuzziness of this "global strobe": globalization understood as an increasing global integration of economies, societies, and cultures through the exchange of products (trade), individuals (transport), and information (technology).

Just as the Flash is one character embodied by many individuals, globalization is also one process encompassing several dimensions. Each scarlet sprinter redefined the word hero by giving the Flash his own specific characteristic. Just as there are one and many Flashes, we can also identify different levels of globalization:

- Focusing exclusively on the commercial level, globalization could more properly be dubbed *internationalization*. This means the increased availability of products in different parts of the world. Apple computers, Coca-Cola drinks, or McDonald's burgers have a global presence and are available from Seattle to Singapore and from Buenos Aires to Beijing. Internationalization also refers to the fact that a product is no longer produced exclusively within the national boundaries of a country; its different parts or stages travel within global value chains that expand across multiple locations.
- The financial side is called *liberalization*, which implies the free movement of capital across borders. This can be through foreign direct investment from one state or company in one country to another or because a person in Venezuela buys bitcoins in a South African web exchange.
- At the consumption level, globalization implies product *uniformity*, which translates into *homogenization* of consumption and consumers. Value is both material and symbolic, pricing and branding. Individuals with the most followers on Instagram in 2021 were Portuguese footballer Cristiano Ronaldo (more than 252 million) and US singer Ariana Grande (215 million). Their fans not only admire their soccer or musical virtues; they seek to internalize an ethical and aesthetic package sold on a global scale and for a global stage: teenagers with haircuts that emulate them can be seen from Manila to Mexico and from New Delhi to New York.
- Globalization also tends to *universalize* values by standardizing the balance between rights and responsibilities, the parameters of equality and hierarchy, the foundations for obedience and authority, and even the notions of freedom and domination (rights of women and children; treatment of ethnic, religious, or sexual minorities).

- Politically, globalization is a process of increasing *de-territorialization*. Nation-states see their exclusive claim to control and authority constantly reduced through an incessant, technologically driven international interpenetration of material and informational flows. National rulers are increasingly conditioned by international factors. At the political level, globalization is not only a process but a deliberate and strategic *project* to consolidate power. Globalization is the supportive structure of ideas and institutions, rules, norms, and behaviors that legitimize the power/domination of the powerful/central states and normalize the acquiescence of the weak/peripheral countries.

- Technologically, globalization represents the *intensification* of scientific progress and global knowledge flows. Globalization has amplified the diffusion of foreign technologies and facilitated access to knowledge generated in other parts of the world. This has enabled a reach and speed to globalization never recorded before in history: 69 million WhatsApp and Facebook Messenger messages were sent in a minute in 2021. In that same minute, 500 hours of video content were uploaded to YouTube; 197.6 million e-mails were sent; there were over 4.1 million Google searches; 200,000 people were tweeting and 28,000 Netflix subscribers watching; 415,000 apps were downloaded; and US$1.6 million was spent online—all in the same minute, a speed worthy of the ruby racer.

In the comic narrative, there is also a Black Flash. He plays the role of death for those with super speed by returning them to the source (the Speed Force). It is not clear if Black Flash exists because the Flash is too fast for death or if it is a side effect of the connection with the Speed Force. In the same way, globalization has a "dark" side, and it is also unclear as to whether it is structural to the process or a negative externality. Interestingly, the Black Flash logo is the same as the Flash logo. It is not even reversed, which would indicate an antihero or villain status. It hints at a structural unity between both. Globalization allows workers or victims of human trafficking to cross borders, Coca-Cola and cocaine to be sold globally, literature or pornography to be uploaded to the Internet. Thus, transnational organized crime is the Black Flash of globalization: the same capabilities, different in values. Drug cartels operate like a multinational company: they offer differentiated products; have structured parent companies and subsidiaries; created logistical networks; have strict policies for recruiting, selecting, and "firing" personnel; and participate in internationalized value chains. The difference is that they do not sell computers or hamburgers but traffic drugs, weapons, people, animal species, and counterfeit goods. In Afghanistan, the United Nations estimated the illicit gross income of the opiate economy to be worth between $1.2 billion and $2.2 billion in 2018, a value corresponding to 6 to 11 percent of the country's gross domestic product that year. This was more than its officially recorded exports of goods and services, estimated at 4.3 percent of GDP.

Transnational organized crime generates between US$1.6 billion and US$2.2 billion annually.[2] Quantifying these markets reveals that this is not a "few bad apples" phenomenon:

The Global Initiative Against Transnational Organized Crime's 2021 report estimated global money laundering to stand at 2.7 percent of global GDP. By vibrating his body at a specific frequency, the Flash—Red or Black—can become intangible, allowing him to pass through solid matter. Globalization also crosses the barriers from the legal to the illegal and vice versa. The overlap between the legal and illegal sides is the result of an inherent tension of global economic expansion. The world's most traditional and reputable investment houses and banks have a symbiotic relation with less reputable international entities: the German Commerzbank processed more than US$250 billion from Sudanese suspected terrorist entities between 2002 and 2008, US Wachovia/Wells Fargo bank laundered US$373 billion from the Mexican Sinaloa cartel, HSBC and Standard Chartered banks processed over US$667 million in suspicious transactions with Iranian and Saudi entities linked to terrorism, Swiss wealth management group Julius Baer laundered US$1.2 billion from embezzled funds from Venezuela's state-owned company PDVSA, and the Danish Danske Bank admitted in 2018 to "suspicious" transactions for US$235 billion with Russian oligarchs. In his novel *The Red and the Black*, French novelist Stendhal juxtaposes the two colors to represent the tension between the army and the clergy. In today's globalization, the Black Flash and the Red Flash seem to have been integrated.

Illegal Market[3]	Estimated Value (USD)
Counterfeit goods	923 billion–1.13 trillion
Drug trafficking	426–652 billion
Timber (logging)	52–157 billion
Trafficking in persons	150 billion
Mining	12–48 billion
Fisheries	15.5–36.4 billion
Wildlife	5–23 billion
Crude oil	5.2–11.9 billion
Small arms and light weapons	1.7–3.5 billion
Organs	840 million–1.7 billion
Cultural property	1.2–1.6 billion

Chapter Eight

Cyborg

The World's Digital Duplicate

Victor Stone was an American football star born in Gotham City. A car accident mutilated most of his body, and he was saved from death by a cybernetic transformation. Reduced to nothing more than his torso, head, and half his arms, he was kept alive by his father, Silas, who tried all kinds of medical procedures to heal him. The last and most desperate attempt was to rebuild his body with technological improvements. In the process, Dr. Stone built a living machine stronger than his host: Cyborg. Part man, part machine, Vic was far stronger than the average person, could interface with computers, and could emit various types of energy. He had cybernetic enhancements that provided him with superhuman intelligence, strength, endurance, and durability. He enjoyed body self-regeneration and could transform parts of his body into technological weapons and equipment (finger laser, infrared eye, telescopic eye, sonic disruptor, electric shocks, electromagnetic pulse cannons). He also had "mechanokinesis" (the ability to mentally control computers, robots, or any technological or mechanical device).

In October 2019, the Internet reached half a century. International relations in the digital age have taken on very specific characteristics. Like the Cyborg, they showcase their usual features (the human part) but are now intertwined with technology (the robotic part). The digital revolution has brought about a profound transformation in contemporary world affairs. Data for 2021[4] showed 4.66 billion people are online (59 percent of total population), a 316 million increase from 2020. Nonetheless, 3.2 billion people worldwide were still offline. The average Internet user will spend 6 hours and 54 minutes online in 2021, more than 100 days in total. Globally, this would amount to a collective total of 1.25 billion years online by 2020, estimated before the global confinement by the COVID-19 pandemic. Around 53.6 percent of the world's population (4.2 billion) now use social networks, an increase of 490 million since 2020. Social platforms have more users than countries' inhabitants: Facebook had in 2021 2,740 million, just under twice the number of the most populous country (China, 1,444 million); WhatsApp has 2 billion and exceeds the second most populous country (India, 1,392 million); WeiXin/WeChat (1,213 million) is almost four times the size of the United States (333 million); Pinterest is roughly the size of the European Union (442 million users and 448 million inhabitants in the EU); Twitter users number 353 million; while Instagram (1.2 billion) exceeds the combined populations of Japan, Russia, Brazil, Mexico, Turkey, Iran, South Korea, Australia, and Indonesia. Digital social networks have not only changed people's methods of communication but are also transforming the way we understand and signify our reality. Manuel Castells (2011) defines them as an interactive system with information disseminated on the Internet by citizens themselves, using it as a documentary source and also organizing groups transmitting directly to mobile phones for free. It is a new mass communication system built as an interactive and multimodal mix between television, Internet, radio, and mobile communication platforms; a cyber-sphere within the biosphere, like Cyborg is a cybernetic organism within Victor.

Digital technologies are the way of perceiving reality: with computer language algorithms, we interpret the world (from weather to traffic conditions); we decide the products we buy; we choose the entertainment we enjoy and connect with the topics we care about or the people we care for.[5] In our COVID-19 era, connectivity ceased to be a convenience and became a necessity. During the successive lockdowns worldwide, almost all human activities—commerce, education, health care, politics, and even socializing—moved into the online realm. At the same time, algorithms driving artificial intelligence (AI) became capable of identifying faces in photos, recognizing written or spoken words, and establishing patterns of consumption and behavior. Like a Cyborg in the cloud, Google knows what we are looking for and when and where we are looking for it—and at a dizzying speed. The fifth generation of cellular networks (5G) will facilitate increased machine operation at wireless connection speeds of up to one hundred times faster than 4G. At a time when communication happens mainly through computer devices, global politics—the international relation between states and the domestic between those states and their citizens—is also critically reshaped. As Cyborg himself states: "Human. Tech. I do not choose sides; I am the bridge between them. I am a cyborg." A digital footprint is the trail of information you leave behind when you use the Internet. Our online activity (posts, publications, likes, chats, e-mails, audio messages, videoconferences, communities) generates an enormous amount of information about who we are, what we think, and whom and what we relate to. This information can be used to deepen freedom of choice by more accurately filtering what we like and dislike. Technological utopianism—or what Morozov (2013) calls "technological solutionism"—assumes that technology will be the basis of future social innovation, deepening democratic governance by increasing transparency and accountability. Eventually, humanity will arrive at a more prosperous, egalitarian, sustainable, healthy, and peaceful society, a horizontal and digital postpower society reminiscent of Aldous Huxley's *Brave New World*: "Community, Identity, Stability." But social networks alone do not and cannot organize societies. They can even facilitate the opposite: a heightened control of information due to state surveillance build-up to limit freedom of expression. Freedom House's *Freedom on the Net 2019* report warns about the growing "digital authoritarianism."[6] The organization noted state and nonstate actors in many countries were exploiting opportunities created by the pandemic to shape online narratives, censor critical speech, and build new technological systems of social control. Digital electoral interference and massive government surveillance of social networks became standard tools for social monitoring and international competition. Virtually all governments used some degree of digital technology to monitor the behavior of their citizens online for the sake of addressing security or the pandemic's public health crisis. Democratic and nondemocratic regimes alike cited CO-VID-19 to justify expanded surveillance powers and the deployment of new technologies once seen as too intrusive. Digitization, collection, and analysis of people's most intimate data were carried out with minimal protections against abuses. Governments, private companies, and security agencies adopted AI, biometric surveillance, and big-data tools to make decisions directly impinging on individuals' economic, social, and political rights without transparency or independent oversight. Cybercriminals now have easy access not only to sensitive personal information but also medical histories (including genetic information) and facial and voice patterns.

An interconnected world has consequences also at the international level. The interpenetration of the digital into the real implies new vulnerabilities for national security that can be exploited by state and nonstate actors. Today a digital duplicate of physical reality has emerged. In addition to land, air, water, and space, cyberspace has been added as another field of human interaction, economic exchange, and competition for power. Cyberspace is problematic for a territorially based political organization like the nation-state. Cyberwar and cyberterrorism allow for exploratory infiltration, unauthorized modification of websites, denial of service (incapacitating or blocking servers), malware attacks, destruction of digital or physical infrastructure, data theft, malicious intervention of public service networks, and hacking and control of unmanned aerial vehicles (UAVs or drones). The market has professionalized, the dark web has matured, and the ease of engaging in criminal activity on the Internet has lowered the threshold for engagement and increased opportunities. Cybercrime and industrial espionage (bank account data or credit card number theft, digital commercial fraud, and identity theft) will cost international companies US\$5.2 trillion between 2019 and 2023. Cyborg-like capabilities exist and are being deployed by governments all over the world. The United States has the National Security Agency (NSA). Together with the Department of Defense's Cybercommand, they created ARES, a secret task force. In November 2016, they launched Operation Glowing Symphony, the largest cyber offensive in US military history. ARES infiltrated accounts of the ISIS terrorist group, deleted content, blocked servers, and disrupted network access. It removed ISIS from cyberspace and deprived it of the main instrument for spreading its message, recruiting, and publicizing its attacks. In the United Kingdom, the 77th Brigade is tasked with carrying out "psychological operations and use of social networks for unconventional warfare in the information age." Another example is Operation Quito, a campaign carried out by the JTRIG (Joint Threat Research Intelligence Group) to prevent Argentina from retaking the Falkland Islands in 2009. Although it is not a seamless dragnet or perfect panopticon, the Chinese government already possesses the most agile, invasive, and omnipresent domestic surveillance capabilities in the world. Members of Unit 61398 of the Chinese People's Liberation Army were accused in the United States of stealing Social Security numbers from more than 145 million Americans, almost half the country's population. The Russian Central Intelligence Department (GRU) and the Federal Security Service (FSB) operate covertly with hacker groups such as Cyber Berkut (which infiltrated the Central Election Commission of Ukraine's website in the postrevolutionary elections) or Turla (which hacked organizations in at least twenty different countries between 2018 and 2019). Cyberattacks are extremely difficult to prevent, detect, and attribute. Groups that are not organically attached to states also appear to act for them, such as the Iranian Cyber Army (ICA) or the Lazarus group (responsible for the attack on Sony in 2014), which acts for the North Korean Bureau 121.

There has always been an overlap between technology and national security. Arthur Schlesinger (1999) interpreted that "science and technology revolutionize our lives, but memory, tradition and myth frame our responses." The rate of fire of a medieval English archer was 12 arrows per minute; the rate of the Browning 0.50-caliber machine-gun of the Second World War was 1,200. Cyborg or the digital duplication of current world affairs is different: artificial intelligence is not just about automation. Its fundamentally disruptive quality rests on its self-learning capability. It gains knowledge through processes constantly changing: it instantly acquires and analyzes new data and seeks to "improve" itself on the basis of that analysis. In June 2021, Google announced a new machine-learning algorithm that worked out where to place the billions of components that a modern computer chip needs. This can take human designers months and failed to be automated. Not only does the algorithm complete the task in a fraction of the time it takes humans, it is already designing Google's next generation of AI processors. AI has the potential to set its own goals. Processes are based on algorithms (mathematical interpretations of observed data) but then AI "learns" by making marginal adjustments to its algorithms. Thus, it can individualize and anticipate results. However, AI learning is mathematical, not conceptual. It does not explain the underlying reality that produces those results. Without the human component, Cyborg would run the risk of misinterpreting human instructions due to an inherent lack of context. Throughout human history, civilizations have created ways to explain the world around them: religion (Middle Ages), reason (modernity), history (nineteenth century), ideology (twentieth century). Victor Stone also wonders what kind of life he is supposed to live now as he reviews the highlights of his high school football days using the projectors in his hands. As Henry Kissinger wondered: will AI's decision-making surpass the explanatory powers of human language and reason? What will become of human consciousness if its own explanatory power is surpassed by AI and societies are no longer able to interpret the world they inhabit in terms that are meaningful to them? How is consciousness to be defined in a world of machines that reduce human experience to mathematical data, interpreted by their own memories? Who is responsible for the actions of artificial intelligence, of a Cyborg without the human anchorage of a Victor Stone? Are we heading toward growing convergence between human beings and technology, a new biological-cybernetic equilibrium? And toward a global politics that integrates the organic and the robotic? Will the international system be increasingly defined as a cyber-physical system due to the integration of computation, networking, and physical processes? Victor himself asks this premonitory question: "Not long ago I wondered whether I had lost my soul, my identity, by becoming a machine, perhaps even a monster. But I was not a monster. I was who I had always been. My soul was still intact. In fact, my soul needed the machine to embark on its journey to the next evolutionary step for humankind. A journey I relished taking, the only way I could, as Cyborg."[7]

Chapter Nine

Peter's Web

International Organizations

International or intergovernmental organizations are the rules that govern world politics and the institutions that uphold those rules in practice. They provide states with a structure of incentives, costs, values, and meanings that define the expected and acceptable behavior for them in the international arena. It is in this they resemble Spider-Man's superpower. Whether they are global (United Nations, World Bank, World Health Organization) or regional (European Union, Arab League, Organization of American States, African Union), they all work like a spider's web. In 2020, there were 7,804 intergovernmental organizations recorded worldwide. The effectiveness of international organizations rests on their ability to move between divergent interests of states and achieve behavior that states alone would not have. Spidey moves between buildings and his power lies in how effective he is at tying up the villain. Spider orb-webs have evolved to intercept, absorb, and dissipate the kinetic energy from prey impact. They retain prey until the spider can subdue it. The web's structure and function depend upon a capture composite material made of supporting fibers covered in sticky glue droplets. Orb-web threads are both adhesive and extensible, and their performance is influenced by ambient conditions. International institutions act exactly like this: their functioning effectiveness depends upon the supporting fibers of the will of nation-states in the international community. Mead (2004) takes up a concept from North (1991) arguing that international economic policies and institutions promoted by the United States act as "sticky power," attracting other countries to its sphere of influence and "trapping" them. International organizations are also adhesive and extensible, binding together common interests to the extent to which they are common.

An hour-and-a-half drive from where Peter Parker lives, Princeton University professor John Ikenberry—the leading mind in neoliberal institutionalism—argues the durability of the liberal international order lies in the ability of its institutions to *bind* and *bond* (Ikenberry, 1999). Repeated interactions provide the motivation for states to create international organizations, and international organizations provide states with a common set of rules for all, irrespective of their relative power. Binding refers to moderating the conduct of states through the framework for interaction, establishing mechanisms to reduce cheating by monitoring or punishing and facilitating transparency. The World Trade Organization developed procedures for making rules, settling disputes, and punishing those who fail to follow the rules. States become socialized through routine bureaucracies and procedures that make intentions visible and reduce misperception or communication mistakes. By prescribing and proscribing behavior, states' expectations are stabilized and competition for power tempered. The UN's International Atomic Energy Agency establishes regularized processes of information gathering, analysis, and surveillance. International institutions provide a different arena for resolving disputes with resources that are not necessarily military: codified principles rather than deployed powers. Brunei, China, Malaysia, the Philippines, and Vietnam have overlapping claims in the South China Sea. The United Nations Convention on the Law of the Sea (UNCLOS) seeks to overcome unilateral action, which would give the more powerful the advantage. The Arctic Council seeks to reduce the risk of future confrontation between powers over territory, routes, and natural resources when sea ice thinning and melting permafrost open up this area for human activity. "Bonding" international organizations are the focal points for global cooperation and coordination. Structured dialogue between nations increases the credibility of commitments and thus establishes a reputation for compliance. By transforming individual states into collective members of an international regime, international organizations enhance the value of a good reputation. Members have an interest in becoming "responsible shareholders" in the international system. That interest is both material and symbolic. The 78,988 UN personnel deployed in the twelve UN peace missions under way in April 2021 were not in the interest of any of the 122 contributing states but rather in the interest of the international community of which those countries are members. The weak state accepts being part of an institutionally mediated order so as not to be at the mercy of blunt force (domination or abandonment). Even if it does not always work in its favor, the hypocrisy of the institutions is preferable to the cynicism of power. Whereas the powerful create and sustain international organizations to mask/maintain domination and because of strategic self-limitation (avoiding the wearing out of resources and legitimacy due to constantly using power), Spidey's dictum is the basis of the institutions driving the American international liberal order: "With great power comes great responsibility."

Spider-Man-like international webs are not limited to international inter-governmental organizations (created and supported by states). Just as Peter can throw individual threads, there are also nonstate actors that are part of the complex global orb-web. These include subnational state actors. They can be state (provinces, municipalities, cities) or nonstate (nongovernmental organizations and transnational companies). Below the central/deferral government we find provinces (for example, Navarra in Spain or Punjab in Pakistan), states (Landtag of Bavaria in Germany, Massachusetts in the United States), municipalities or communes (Montelepre in Sicily, Italy), and cities (Los Angeles in California, United Sates). Each country organizes their administrative political division in different tiers with names that can be at one level in one of them and in a higher or lower level of hierarchy in another. For example, Bolivia's 112 provinces are the second level of organization (the first level are its nine departments) while for Canada and China, their ten and twenty-three provinces represent their first tier of political division. Whatever their classification, all subnational levels have gained greater international autonomy and do not always act in harmony with the central state. Often their local interests clash with the national interest. The case of cities is especially relevant. While in the international system, we can identify less than two hundred governments, UN Habitat estimated in 2020 there were 34 metropolises with more than 10 million inhabitants; 51 with a population of 5 to 10 million; 494 of 1 to 5 million; and 1,355 of 300,000 to 1 million. In total, there were 1,934 metropolises with more than 300,000 inhabitants in the world in 2020, representing approximately 60 percent of the world's urban population. At least 2.59 billion people lived in metropolises in 2020, which is equivalent to one-third of the global population. Tokyo is the largest city in the world with a population of 37 million. It is followed by Delhi with 29 million; Shanghai with 26 million; Mexico City and São Paulo with about 22 million inhabitants; and Cairo, Mumbai, Beijing, and Daca with about 20 million inhabitants.[8] In 2010 the world became 51 percent urban for the first time in history. In 2019 it reached 56 percent and is expected to reach 68 percent by 2050 (United Nations, 2019). Cities and metropolitan areas or urban agglomerations contribute about 60 percent of the world's GDP. They also account for 70 percent of global carbon emissions and over 60 percent of resource use. Only three countries—India, China, and Nigeria—will contribute 35 percent of urban population growth to 2050. Spider-Man is an urban superhero, facing the challenges of a crime fighter while dealing with the dilemmas of the average teenager living in Queens. In fact, the comic is not set in a fictional city like Gotham or Metropolis. Peter Parker has the urban setting, over which he has no control, as a framework for his actions. It interacts with an "imposed" urban reality. Similarly, the most pressing issues on the current global agenda (pollution, housing, poverty, economic development, technological innovation) are "imposed" on cities first.

The Organization for Economic Co-operation and Development (OECD, 2018) estimated that transnational or multinational[9] enterprises or corporations (MNEs or MNCs) account for 70 percent of world trade, 50 percent of world exports, 28 percent of world GDP, and 23 percent of global employment. In knowledge-intensive goods sectors, MNCs make up as much as 90 percent of exports. Their transnational activities have transformed the nature of trade, investment, and technology transfer in globalization. The extensive global value chains (GVCs) that structure today's world economy have been driven by the way MNCs structure their global operations through outsourcing and offshoring activities. There are around eight thousand MNCs worldwide. Even with the recession from the COVID-19 global pandemic, Apple's market capitalization in 2020 made it the twenty-fourth largest economy in the world. ExxonMobil was almost as big as the entire economy of Angola, and Facebook was twice the size of Finland. Côte d'Ivoire provides 44 percent of the world's cocoa, but its economy is half the valuation of Nestlé. The luxury brand company LVMH is ten times the GDP of Haiti, and the combined GDPs of Bolivia and Paraguay are less than Coca-Cola's valuation. The total valuation of Google is over US$1.6 trillion, and only twelve countries have more GDP than the tech giant. Amazon earns more money than 92 percent of countries of the world. These companies are actors with political influence in the formulation of national public policies, such as taxation and immigration. The last thread in this orb-web of nonstate actors are nongovernmental organizations (NGOs). The term NGO was created in Article 71 of the United Nations Charter for any type of organization that is independent of government influence and not for profit. NGOs do not possess attributes of military strength or territorial control. But they do form transnational networks of advocacy and influence. This global civil society is constituted by organizations such as Greenpeace, Red Cross International, Freedom House, Human Rights Watch, Amnesty International, Oxfam, and Doctors without Borders. The *Yearbook of International Organizations 2020* tallied 65,027 international NGOs (exclusively national civil society organizations exceed 10 million). There are also a similar number of transnational coalitions of social movements and scientific communities. We tend to associate NGOs with humanitarian groups working for a greater social, environmental, economic, or political good. However, NGOs can also form a "global uncivil society" such as international organized crime, international drug cartels, and terrorist groups like Al-Qaeda. This "Injustice League" is made up of global terrorist groups and transnational organized crime. The same channels of globalization that enable McDonald's to have 38,000 premises in more than 100 countries and reach 69 million customers daily enable the Sicilian mafia to reach Uruguay, the United States, South Africa, and Southeast Asia. Like

Venom in Sam Raimi's *Spider-Man 3*, NGOs can be like Peter Parker (virtuous) or Eddie Brock (vile).

Part III

Why We Fight

Global Issues

After reviewing international relations theoretical lenses (the how) and the composition of global structure (the where), we identify now the main issues (the what) in the global agenda. The initial issues of war and trade that dominated international relations have now been reformulated and extended to include conflict resolution; peacekeeping; human rights protection; international justice; the promotion of economic development and social progress; nuclear proliferation; transnational terrorism; public health threats; economic inequality; the interacting, combined effects of climate change, resource scarcity, and environmental degradation; disaster relief; education and advancement of women; and the peaceful uses of atomic energy.

Chapter Ten

War

Tony Stark, Iron Man, and the Military-Industrial Complex

In his 1961 farewell speech, US President Dwight Eisenhower warned against a future in which a powerful military-industrial complex would manipulate policy to the detriment of US national interests. Two years later, Iron Man appeared, a vehicle for Stan Lee to explore the role of American technology and industry in the fight against communism. Iron Man is Anthony "Tony" Edward Stark, a brilliant scientist and billionaire tycoon of the arms industry. While consulting on a weapons contract overseas, he is kidnapped in enemy terrain. Awakening as a prisoner of the warlord Wong-Chu, Tony makes a gruesome discovery: the explosion had sent a piece of shrapnel mere inches from his heart. It was only the timely intervention of fellow captive and engineer Yinsen that kept the shrapnel at bay. His captors try to force him to build a weapon of mass destruction. Combining their genius, Tony and Yinsen build a mighty iron armor suit, Iron Man. Yinsen sacrifices his life, and Tony escapes wearing the mechanized armor. Once returned to the United States, Tony adds weapons and other technological devices through his company, Stark Industries, and dedicates his life to fighting threats to the world. He uses the suit and successive versions to protect the world as Iron Man. Although at first he hid his true identity, Stark finally reveals he is Iron Man in a very narcissistic public announcement.

According to the Stockholm International Peace Research Institute (SIPRI 2021), international arms transfers remain close to the highest level since the end of the Cold War. Arms sales by the world's twenty-five largest arms-producing and military services companies (arms companies) totaled US$361 billion. Twelve US companies appeared in the top twenty-five, and the top five companies were all based in the United States: Lockheed Martin, Boeing, Northrop Grumman, Raytheon, and General Dynamics. Together, they registered $166 billion in annual arms sales. The twelve American companies accounted for 61 percent of the combined arms sales of the top twenty-five. After the United States, China accounted for the second-largest share with 16 percent and four companies: Aviation Industry Corporation of China (AVIC), China Electronics Technology Group Corporation (CETC), China North Industries Group Corporation (NORINCO), and China South Industries Group Corporation (CSGC). The six Western European companies together accounted for 18 percent, and the two Russian companies (Almaz-Antey and United Shipbuilding) in the ranking accounted for 3.9 percent. The United States remains the largest arms exporter, increasing its global share to 37 percent and supplying major arms to ninety-six states. Almost half (47 percent) of US arms transfers went to the Middle East, and Saudi Arabia alone accounted for 24 percent of total US arms exports. The second-largest arms exporter was Russia, which accounted for 20 percent of global major arms sales. The third-largest exporter was France, with 8.2 percent of global arms exports, mainly to India, Egypt, and Qatar (59 percent of French arms exports). Germany accounted for 5.5 percent of the global total. The top markets for German arms exports were South Korea, Algeria, and Egypt. In 2020, US military expenditure reached US$778 billion, representing 39 percent of total expenditure. This was the third consecutive year of growth in US military spending, following seven years of continuous reductions. China's military expenditure was the second-highest in the world at an estimated US$252 billion in 2020. This is a 76 percent increase over the decade 2011–2020. China's military spending has risen for twenty-six consecutive years. World military spending rose to almost US$2 trillion in 2020 (US$1,981 billion), or US$254 per person in the world.

What is war? Roman statesman Marcus Tullius Cicero called it "a contention by force." British philosopher Thomas Hobbes understood war in an attitudinal sense: "a state of affairs, which may exist even while its operations are not continued." A symbol of the eighteenth-century Enlightenment, French philosopher Denis Diderot described war as "the fruit of man's depravity; it is a convulsive and violent sickness of the body politic." Baron Karl von Clausewitz's (1976) more realist definition is closer to an instrument of public policy: "War is the continuation of politics by other means." Underlying each definition are particular political or philosophical positions. For example, Clausewitz's political theory implies that wars are an inherent part of international politics; they only involve states. Rousseau also argues from this political-rational view of warfare, when he states, "War then is a relation, not between man and man, but between State and State." This school of thought centered on rational, unitary states cannot qualify prestate or nonstate confrontations as wars. Hegelian philosophy would define war as an all-pervasive phenomenon of the universe since change (physical, social, political, economic) can only arise out of war or violent conflict. Operationally, there are three accepted standards in international relations. First, war is organized, deliberate violence by an identifiable political authority. Riots, for example, even if lethal, are not considered war. Second, wars are relatively more lethal than other forms of organized violence. Purges, pogroms, and massacres are deliberate and organized but in general do not have the scale to count as war. Currently, the threshold is at least one thousand deaths in a calendar year for an event to count as a war. Third, war requires at least two actors capable of harming each other, although that capacity need not be equal. This rules out genocides, massacres, ethnic cleansing, and terrorist attacks because one side has real capacity to kill.

What are wars like? There are many criteria for classifying war. The broadest one is dependent on where are they fought: wars that occur between sovereign states (interstate war) and wars that happen within states (intrastate war). The former pit two states against each other, such as the war between China and Japan (Second Sino-Japanese War, 1937–1945) or the war between Iraq and Iran (First Persian Gulf War, 1980–1988). Intrastate wars are called *civil wars* and occur within states. In intrastate wars, ethnic, religious, or political factions battle against each other. Since the end of the Second World War, *interstate* wars have decreased in frequency and severity, while *intrastate* wars have increased. Recent examples are the civil wars in Libya (February–October 2011), Ukraine (2014), and Syria (June 2012–present). In the superhero universe, Iron Man takes part in the "Intra-Avengers" Civil War. When the US government introduced a "Living Weapon of Mass Destruction" registry for all superpowered individuals, Tony Stark and Steve Rogers found themselves on opposite sides. Captain America refused to sign it or to apprehend rogue heroes. He believed heroes needed to be above direct government control. Iron Man, on the other hand, felt superheroes should have oversight beyond casual self-policing and gathered his own pro-registration heroes to bring in Captain America's faction and other nonregistered super combatants.

Wars can also be classified by aims and means. Here we distinguish between total and limited wars. Total wars involve the major powers in the system, applying all their national resources and available means of destruction in pursuit of ultimate objectives (occupation, unconditional surrender, destruction). The Thirty Years' War (1618–1648) was the longest total war ever fought, involving the great powers of the time (England, France, the Habsburg, Austria, the Dutch Republic, Spain, and Sweden) and resulting in more two million deaths on the battlefield. The First and Second World Wars also involved the great powers of the time (Britain, France, Austria-Hungary, Germany, Japan, Russia/USSR, and the United States) and were fought in all spaces (land, air, and water), on all continents, and with all possible means (from bullets to nuclear bombs). The results were dramatic: Germany disappeared as a state until 1990, and casualties were more than thirty-seven million for the First and around seventy-five million for the Second. *Avengers: Infinity War* is a (super)example of an all-out war: the Avengers, the Masters of the Mystic Arts, the Guardians of the Galaxy, and the armed forces of Wakanda challenge Thanos's mad crusade to wipe out half of the universe through the collection of all six Infinity Stones. Limited wars are limited in the number of actors, means, and ends. During the Malvinas/Falklands War between Argentina and the United Kingdom in 1982, neither London nor Buenos Aires were bombed, nor was any action taken outside the South Atlantic.

Finally, wars can be divided into conventional and unconventional, according to their character or how they are fought. Conventional in war means two distinct groups of professional soldiers, a clearly identifiable battlefield, and weapons whose effects apply to the specific time and space of the confrontation. Any fact that bends these three characteristics moves the conflict into the unconventional category. An unconventional confrontation is not between two enemies of equivalent kind (two conventional armies) but enemies of different degree (one with greater power than the other) or different in nature (like a nation-state and a terrorist transnational organization). In the past, battles took place far from urban centers: Thermopylae, Gettysburg, Waterloo, El Alamein. Current-day war is fought mainly in cities: Sarajevo, Mogadishu, Fallujah, Aleppo. This blurs the line between civilian and military. Technologically, nuclear, chemical, and biological weapons have effects that persist over time and are impossible to limit to the field of battle. In unconventional or asymmetric conflict, one of the parties is weaker. However, instead of not resorting to warfare for being successfully deterred, the weak party wages war in an irregular manner by exploiting the stronger party's weakness. Guerrilla warfare is an example. The Irish IRA attacked the British army with the same logic as Batman's campaign against Superman: with a series of traps and kryptonite weapons (in the form of gas and on the tip of a spear) that allow Batman to reduce the asymmetry of power with Superman in order to inflict damage.

Why are there wars? Superhero narratives do not question the causes of war; they merely provide a validation of the war experience. Sometimes they give an answer to the question of a particular conflict, war in the singular. There is always someone that wants to dominate: Earth, the Galaxy, the Universe, the Multiverse. In the same way, for international relations, human nature is assumed to be selfish, ambitious, self-interested, and constantly in pursuit of power. The fatal result is "Homo homini lupus" (man is a wolf to man), as the Latin proverb goes. A variant of this explanation is not human nature itself but the nature of certain humans who by psychological disposition have an insatiable thirst for domination and a penchant for violence: war as the result of sadist psychopaths (Idi Amin of Uganda or the Joker) or vengeful sociopaths (Adolf Hitler, Lex Luthor, Caligula, Darkseid, Pol Pot, Thanos, Nero, Magneto, or Joseph Stalin). The superhero-supervillain confrontation is perpetual because the existence of wickedness is imperishable.

A second explanation is that wars arise due to misperceptions or misinformation and the consequent miscalculations. When actions are misjudged or intentions misinterpreted, mistrust of the other side increases. This gives rise to a "security dilemma" (Jervis, 1978). A state's security is ensured only by its accumulating military and economic power. However, when a state seeks to improve its own security, it is automatically interpreted by another state as threatening since one state's accumulation makes other states less secure. Tragically, steps pursued by states to improve their security have unintended and unforeseen effects. Tension and conflict can arise between states even when they do not intend them, and spiraling suspicion can get out of control and lead to confrontation. A real-world example was the Cold War nuclear arms race. Although both sides could have done more to assuage their enemies' fears of nuclear monopoly, it is hard to imagine any reasonable efforts that would have convinced any of them to forgo nuclear weapons. A security dilemma appears in the absence of a supranational authority, when there is no Superman. We can observe it in the superhero world of relative balance of power, like in *The Avengers* saga. In the 2012 film Tony Stark, Thor, and Nick Fury discuss the security dilemma:

Thor: Your work with the tesseract[10] is what drew Loki to it . . . and his allies. It is a signal to the Realm that Earth is ready for a higher form of war!

Nick Fury: Higher form? You forced our hand! We had to come up with some way that we could . . .

Tony Stark: A nuclear deterrent? 'Cause that always works well . . .

Thor explains how, in their attempt to build a defensive weapon, humans had walked right into war with the Realm. Thor's arrival on Earth (referring to the film *Thor*, 2011) critically transformed the notion of insecurity for Earth as a whole. Logically, S.H.I.E.L.D.[11] launched the Tesseract harnessing program. Nonetheless, the Realm did not see it as earthling insecurity and a desperate attempt at survival in the face of never-before-seen powers like the ones the Norse god paraded. The Realm—from its own viewpoint—interpreted it as preparation for war.

A third explanation for war is the "liberal triad." The political one ("interdemocratic peace theory") argues that the inherent characteristics of republican regimes make them less prone to war. Governments based on laws (con-

stitutions) are subject to checks and balances (division of powers) and thus
are less likely to resort to war. The decision goes through several institutional
instances that make it more difficult. Democratic governments have periodic,
free, transparent, and competitive elections. Elected representatives must
weigh the chances of succeeding in war against the probability of continuity
in office. The economic explanation ("economic interdependence") assumes
economically integrated states have less incentive for armed confrontation
because being a partner is more beneficial than being an enemy. This is a
crucial hypothesis for understanding current global stability: the economic
relation between the United States and China acts as a moderating force in
the competition for global supremacy. For Washington, attacking Chinese
territory militarily would be like attacking its own territory: US companies in
China would see their operations disrupted and their profits reduced. Thomas
Friedman popularized this insight with his "Golden Arches Theory of Conflict Prevention": no two countries that had McDonald's restaurants would
go to war. The institutional explanation argues that an international system
governed by global liberal institutions reduces the likelihood of armed conflict by providing instances for dialogue and negotiation. Even if there is war,
institutions regulate it with rules and conventions. Think about the battle
between Superman and General Zod as depicted in the 1980 Richard Lester
film or in the 2013 Zack Snyder version. *Superman II* wages war with institutions: Zod is vanquished but by his own undoing, falling into an abyss.
Superman flies with the American flag to restore the roof of the White
House, which had been usurped by Zod. He looks at the American president
and declares: "Good afternoon, Mr. President. Sorry I've been away so long.
I won't let you down again." In *Man of Steel*, Superman breaks Zod's neck.
He then falls to his knees and cries out in regret. He embraces Lois as she
comes in to comfort him. He knows he has just won a fight through force
rather than achieved victory through virtue. Without institutions, even for
Superman, anything goes.

The fourth reason for war is the state. Warring factions seek to gain
territorial control and the resource extraction benefits that come with being
the legitimate authority. Many civil wars have been fought over which
groups, ideologies, and leaders should control a state's government, such as
the Salvadoran civil war (1979–1992), which pitted the Salvadoran Armed
Forces against the insurgent forces of the Farabundo Martí National Liberation Front (FMLN), or the American Civil War (1861–1865) between the
Unionists of the North and the Confederates of the South. The economic side
argues that the need of the capitalist states to provide themselves with material resources, a place for products, conquered markets, or export capital
means that the central states must expand. The conquest of America (1492,
for gold, silver, and spices) or the First and Second Iraq wars (2003, for oil)

would constitute examples of a mercantilist imperialism interpretation of war.

The fifth and final explanation of the war is the international structure. It is also twofold: order or (dis)order. The order explanation stresses the fact that there is no hierarchy or higher authority in the system. This condition is what international relations refers to as "anarchic." Since everyone must survive on their own and there is nothing to prevent war, armed conflict is as tragic and unpreventable as hurricanes and earthquakes. Thomas Hobbes argued that whenever men live without a common power that keeps them all in fear, they are in a condition of war: "every man against every man." Importantly, war is not the same thing as battle or constant fighting but the state in which war remains *possible*. Hobbes likened this situation to the relationship between climate and weather: it may not rain every day, but in some climates, rain is much more common than in others. The one climate preventing war would be the superiority of superheroes. The (dis)order explanation understands it is not only mismatched material power that can mire states into war. In times of "hegemonic transition," there is a deep redistribution of power that increases uncertainty, instability, and the probability of war between declining and rising power. Anticipation of shifts in the relative balance of power (system change) leads to war because more power leads to expectations of more influence, wealth, and security. A challenger might launch a war to accelerate its rise or an established hegemon launch a preventive war to keep a rising challenger from getting stronger.

Once we are done explaining war, then the question remains: what is peace? Some explanations take a minimal definition: "negative peace" is the absence of war or systematic collective physical violence between political communities. "Positive peace" is a long-term process aimed at achieving the absence of indirect or structural violence. This comprehensive definition includes not only the absence of physical violence but also economic violence. At the broadest sense, it includes social integration, shared values, and even harmony or love of humanity—quite a challenge for times in which the general global trend is toward more complex, multidimensional (military, political, economic, and social), high-tech, highly automated, and high-speed warfare. The computerized and increasingly AI nature of military affairs, the sophistication in weapons systems, and the more aggressive military doctrines of the most powerful countries are becoming dangerously intertwined. Perhaps it is as Tony defines it in *Iron Man* (2008): "It's an imperfect world, but it's the only one we got. I guarantee you the day weapons are no longer needed to keep the peace, I'll start making bricks and beams for baby hospitals. . . . My old man had a philosophy: peace means having a bigger stick than the other guy."

Chapter Eleven

Doomsday Clock

Nuclear Proliferation

Nuclear weapons are the supreme manifestation of military power. The energy of a nuclear explosion is released in a number of different ways: an explosive blast, nuclear radiation, thermal radiation (which takes the form of visible light), pulses of electrical and magnetic energy (electromagnetic pulse), and a variety of radioactive particles thrown up into the air by the blast (radioactive fallout). A one-megaton (Mt) nuclear weapon produces a fireball that reaches its peak energy output in ten seconds and can produce temperatures of about one hundred million degrees Celsius at its center, about five times that which occurs at the center of the sun. The thermal pulse burns everything within a radius of thirteen kilometers of the impact site. The blast wave creates a bubble of burning compressed air that expands faster than the speed of sound. The intense light and heat can set simultaneous fires over vast areas of surrounding terrain. These fires, once initiated, heat large volumes of air near the Earth's surface. As heated air buoyantly rises, cool air beyond the burning area rushes in to replace it. Fire winds reach hurricane speeds accompanied by the release of large amounts of potentially lethal toxic smoke and combustion gases. Within the fireball radius, anything inside is effectively vaporized: heavily built concrete buildings are severely destroyed and fatalities approach 100 percent. But different outer circles can be traced with different effects. In an eighty-kilometer radius, radioactive fallout causes burns and, over time, radiation-related illnesses. Of course, these numbers depend on the power of each bomb. For example, the one dropped over Hiroshima was fifteen kilotons; "Fat Boy" over Nagasaki was twenty.[12] The Russian Tsar bomb of 1961 had fifty megatons (equivalent to 2,500 Nagasaki events) and a cloud ten times higher. North Korea's nuclear tests in 2017 were estimated at 150 kilotons. Recent nuclear developments have focused on smaller weapons that are much more precise and equally or more destructive, with around twenty times the power of Hiroshima but only the size of a trashcan.

In 1947, scientists from the University of Chicago who had helped develop the first atomic weapons in the Manhattan Project[13] created the Doomsday Clock, a universally recognized indicator of the world's vulnerability to catastrophe from nuclear weapons. It uses the imagery of apocalypse (*midnight*) and the contemporary idiom of nuclear explosion (*countdown to zero*) to convey the threat level to humanity and the planet. The Doomsday Clock is set every year by the Bulletin of the Atomic Scientists' Science and Security Board. In January 2021, the minute hand was closer than ever before: one hundred seconds to midnight. *Doomsday Clock* is also a sequel to the *Watchmen* comic by Alan Moore and Dave Gibbons. An iconic character in Watchmen is Dr. Manhattan (in obvious reference to the program), who was once a nuclear physicist named Jon Osterman. An accident locked him in an "intrinsic field subtractor" chamber that disintegrated him. As months go by, blue particles[14] and body parts appear floating in the lab until Osterman materializes fully formed as a pure energy creature: Dr. Manhattan, a quantum-based superhero that can apparently exist outside of space and time, teleporting and dividing itself into several different copies. This "supreme superhero" symbolizes the "absolute weapon," as Brodie et al. (1946) described nuclear weapons. Manhattan engraved on his own forehead the molecular structure of hydrogen. World War II weapons used fission, the process of splitting an atom. By the 1950s, the United States had figured out how to harness the power of fusion in bombs as well, making them much more powerful. Hydrogen or thermonuclear bombs are one thousand times more powerful than nuclear ones.[15]

During the Cold War, a peak of 70,300 nuclear weapons was reached in the world (in 1986). The number of nuclear weapons in the world has decreased significantly since then, to an estimated combined total of 13,080 nuclear weapons at the start of 2021. There are nine nuclear-armed states in the world: the United States, Russia, the United Kingdom, France, China, India, Pakistan, Israel, and the Democratic People's Republic of Korea. However, Russia and the United States together possess 93 percent of the global nuclear weapons stockpile, extensive and expensive production facilities, and programs to replace and modernize their arsenal plus missile and aircraft delivery systems. Both are estimated to have had around fifty more nuclear warheads in operational deployment at the start of 2021 than a year earlier. Moscow also increased its overall military nuclear stockpile by around 180 warheads, mainly due to deployment of more multi-warhead land-based intercontinental ballistic missiles (ICBMs) and sea-launched ballistic missiles (SLBMs). The remaining seven nuclear-armed states are also either developing or deploying new weapon systems or have announced their intention to do so; they are increasing the importance they attribute to nuclear weapons in their national security strategies and investing in future capabilities. The overall global number of nukes currently deployed with operational forces is 3,825. The UK's "Integrated Review of Security, Defence, Development and Foreign Policy 2021" reversed a policy of reducing the country's nuclear arsenal (currently 225 warheads) and raised its planned ceiling for nuclear weapons from 180 to 260. China (350) is in the middle of a significant modernization and expansion of its nuclear weapon inventory. India (156) and Pakistan (165) are also expanding their nuclear arsenals, while North Korea (40–50) continues to enhance its military nuclear program as a central element of its national security strategy. France and Israel continued at 290 and 90 warheads.

Nuclear weapons are not only different in degree. They are qualitatively different: they are the first weapons developed not to be used. How does that work? They generate deterrence, provided both states have them. A war between two nuclear states would probably result in the destruction of both. In the Cold War, this deterrence stalemate in which each side acted with increased caution was called "mutually assured destruction" (MAD). In *Watchmen*, Manhattan is used as the absolute deterrent. But would it work against a suicidal terrorist group that had a nuclear weapon? Today there is a risk as disturbing as Rorschach's mind: the specter of nuclear terrorism. For Graham Allison (2018), the cumulative probability of a successful nuclear terrorist attack by 2023 is greater than 85 percent. The spread of unconventional weapons (nuclear, chemical, and biological) is a threat to global security. On current trends, the number of nuclear-weapon states is likely to continue to increase in the coming years, at a rate of one or two nations per decade. This could accelerate if a Middle Eastern country were to develop nuclear weapons. The technology has spread around the world with greater speed and range than ever before. In addition, the difficulty and cost of access have fallen to the lowest levels in history. Nuclear weapons were dropped from fighter planes, ships, or submarines by means of missiles (intercontinental or cruise ballistic). Building a missile or a bomber that can launch a nuclear warhead is a significant engineering feat, which today no more than thirty countries are capable of achieving. These capabilities were once the exclusive purview of a nation-state's defense establishment. But know-how was commercialized (Pakistan[16]), and missile sales became widespread (the Soviet short-range Scuds enabled many countries to learn how to reproduce, modify, and improve them to produce their own version). There is also a cheap alternative available: "dirty bombs."[17] This radioactive bomb does not cause a catastrophe of the same order of destructive magnitude as the A-bomb. Radioactivity spread by dirty bombs is unlikely to be lethal. But it would create panic and mass evacuation. In addition, it would have high decontamination and relocation costs. The probability of a terrorist group detonating a dirty bomb is much higher than that of a group obtaining an improvised nuclear weapon. More than one hundred countries house radiological sources used to power batteries, industrial gauges, or blood irradiation equipment. These isotopes used for life-saving blood transfusions and cancer treatments in hospitals can also be used to build a radiological bomb. Moreover, the facilities where these materials are kept—particularly cesium-137—are poorly secured and vulnerable to theft. Radioactive isotopes are used in dozens of applications, from cancer treatment to pipeline welding inspections, and thousands of packages containing small amounts of radioactive material are shipped each year. In 2016, the Belgian State Security Service (VSSE) discovered terrorists monitoring an employee at a highly enriched uranium reactor that produces medical isotopes for much of Europe.

It would be easy to argue that Dr. Manhattan symbolizes the nuclear threat on the grounds that governments clearly see him in the comic book as a weapon of deterrence that prevents nuclear war. But this would be an oversimplification or a misreading. In fact, it is Ozymandias who promotes the misreading of Manhattan as a nuclear threat because he sees him as an impediment to his plans. Ozymandias exposes several people close to Manhattan to radiation so that they develop cancer and blame it on Dr. Blue. Manhattan does not represent nuclear weapons but the human feelings about them: bewilderment, fear, pride. In his *Duino Elegies*, Bohemian-Austrian poet Rainer Maria Rilke describes "terrifying angels" as one would the age of nuclear weapons or Dr. Manhattan's relation to humankind: "the beginning of terror, which we still are just able to endure, and we are so awed because it serenely disdains to annihilate us."[18]

Chapter Twelve

Lex Luthor and Victor von Doom

Global Inequality

Let me tell you about the very rich. They are different from you and me. They possess and enjoy early, and it does something to them, makes them soft where we are hard, and cynical where we are trustful, in a way that, unless you were born rich, it is very difficult to understand. They think, deep in their hearts, that they are better than we are because we had to discover the compensations and refuges of life for ourselves. Even when they enter deep into our world or sink below us, they still think that they are better than we are. They are different.

This "Rich Boy" described by Francis Scott Fitzgerald in 1926 was Anson Hunter. But the description also fits Lex Luthor, Victor von Doom, Wilson Fisk (Kingpin), and Adrian Veidt (Ozymandias).

The Credit Suisse 2020 *Global Wealth Report* finds household wealth to be "very unevenly" distributed. Geographically, North America and Europe accounted for 55 percent of total global wealth but only 17 percent of the world adult population. The wealth share of these two continents was three times the wealth share in Latin America, four times the wealth share in India, and nearly ten times the wealth share in Africa. Wealth differences within countries are even more pronounced. The top 1 percent of wealth holders in a country typically own 25–40 percent of all wealth, and the top 10 percent usually account for 55–75 percent. Although millionaires worldwide are exactly 1 percent of the adult population, they account for 43.4 percent of *all* global wealth. In contrast, the 54 percent of adults whose net worth is below US$10,000 can muster less than 2 percent of global wealth. The Oxfam 2020 report estimated 2,153 billionaires in the world possess more combined wealth than 4.6 billion people. There are 162 billionaires whose combined wealth exceeds half of humanity (four from the same family, the Walton family, who own Walmart). The richest 1 percent of the world has more than twice the wealth of 6.9 billion people. And if everyone sat on their accumulated wealth in US$100 notes, the majority of humanity would be sitting on the floor. But the two richest men—Jeff Bezos[19] and Bill Gates—would be sitting in outer space. In 2021, Oxfam noted that the *increase* in the wealth of the ten richest billionaires during the COVID-19 pandemic was more than enough to prevent anyone on Earth from falling into poverty and pay for a COVID-19 vaccine for all.

Until around 1800, today's developed world was as poor as today's worst-off places with even worse child mortality. Inequality increased from 1820 to about 1990. This long period of rising inequality was driven by divergences in growth processes. Today's so-called developed world took off economically in the early nineteenth century, with some late entrants such as Japan. The consequent large cross-country differences in improvements in health and economic growth over the past two centuries created the current global inequalities. In the film *Justice League* (2017), it is Luthor who discovers the Flash in his search for metahumans by reviewing videos from a business security camera. Batman also uses these files to find him. The fallen angel of Metropolis and Gotham's bat both predicate their "super" status on their enormous income disparity. An average Swiss citizen can spend in one month what his equivalent in the Central African Republic can spend in seven years. Inequality in living conditions ranges through a number of aspects like health (1 out of 10 children born in Africa will die before they are five years old, but only 1 in 250 born in East Asia) and education (school life expectancy in Australia is 22 but only 9 in Haiti). Global inequalities in health, wealth, education, and other dimensions are outcome inequalities: living conditions are much more dependent on factors outside individual control. In time, these create inequalities of opportunity, inhibiting people's own effort, dedication, and choices to render them a happy, healthy life. If a villain kills your parents but you are wealthy, you can become Batman. However, if you are orphaned by the mob but you are not rich, the most you can aspire to is to become his sidekick, like in Dick Grayson's case. In the current world, this would be developed and emerging countries. The globalization of inequality is manifested in the advanced countries under the criticism that the gains of globalization have not been evenly distributed. Outsourcing has destroyed domestic jobs and livelihoods of entire communities. Workers have experienced stagnant or falling standards of living while the rich get richer. Middle and lower-middle classes in the developed world have seen little or no gain from globalization, while the developing countries have seen substantial gains. The middle classes in Brazil, China, and India have been the big winners from globalization, while the poor and middle classes in Arkansas (US), Cornwall (UK), or Zawadzkie (Poland) have been the big losers. Politically, this fueled movements such as Brexit in the United Kingdom, Lega in Italy, and Make America Great Again in the United States. Interestingly, many of the leaders in this twenty-first-century right-wing populism are themselves wealthy. At the same time, globalization has generated economic growth in initially poor countries. These higher growth rates observed in emerging countries have been best exemplified by the rise of China. And since they year 2000, the entire developing world have seen most of their economies grow significantly. This is why the link in the global south between globalization and inequality goes through growth first. While trade openness is on average (not always) a significant predictor of growth, its empirical relation with inequality is less clear. As economies (in this case, developing ones) become more capitalist, they tend initially to higher levels of inequality (Piketty, 2014). Within countries, inequality increases as their economies grow, but after a point, it peaks and falls. Trade has contributed to promoting growth and poverty reduction in the developing world as a whole, but not in all cases and only as one in a number of relevant factors. Whether capitalism is increasing inequality or not also depends on initial conditions such as factor endowment distribution, regulations, institutional strength, governance structure, and political economy structure. Why did political leaders in Latin America, Africa, and Eastern Europe adopt drastic and costly neo-liberal policies in some countries but not in others? Why did these painful measures gain popular support in some nations while triggering rejection and protest in others? The same question was asked in early 2020 under the global coronavirus pandemic to make governmental decisions about social distancing/quarantine, taking into account their impact on economic growth.

Inequality exposes and questions the nexus between economics and politics, corporations and government, prosperity and power, importance and influence. The "power elite" (Wright Mills, 1956) or "superclass" (Rothkopf, 2008) are no more than six thousand people who exert international political influence based on their economic importance. They are not just a list of individuals with exorbitant fortunes. Wealth is not "natural" but "social," in other words, a result of social processes. And villains personify this social embeddedness aspect in a stark way: why does Norman Osborn become the Green Goblin instead of enjoying his estimated US$10 billion in wealth? The Kingpin has a net worth of well over US$40 billion and control of the criminal underworld. Yet, he becomes the mayor of New York City. To society, Lex Luthor is the pinnacle of human achievement: a respectable, self-made billionaire industrialist with a good standing in the worlds of business and politics. But to Superman he is a dangerous, scheming supervillain. So powerful is the impulse to naturalize wealth neutrality that *Forbes* magazine has a list of the "fictional millionaires" ranging from *The Simpsons'* Montgomery Burns to Tony Stark and from *Lord of the Rings'* Smaug the dragon to Bruce Wayne.[20] They are a socioeconomic stratum more powerful than any state, with autonomous power and in conflict with constitutional and democratic principles such as freedom, representation, and accountability. Wealthy supervillains are not content to enjoy their wealth; they want to dominate the world. The world superclass exercises power by setting the global agenda. Inequality is only the economic manifestation of a growing concentration of power by a shrinking minority. The estrangement of the rich from the common good is reinforced by globalization, which undermines civic duty, separates social classes, and empowers corporations at the expense of governments. In this power constellation, elites are a significant determinant of the behavior of the international system. Globalization has facilitated a combination of hierarchies across different institutional orders that fuses the corporate elite and political leadership into a transnational network of domestic power structures that replicate themselves at the global level, making the national-international distinction irrelevant. LexCorp is not just a company but a platform to finance the election of Luthor to become president of the United States after Bill Clinton (instead of George W. Bush) in 2001. Would it make a difference if the plutocrat running for office was in fact Tony Stark, as President Obama suggests in an episode of the *Civil War* comic book? Inequality symbolizes the relation between wealth and power, market and state, gold and bronze. Dr. Doom claims the nation of Latveria for himself, and King T'Challa (Black Panther) rules Wakanda. Is this explained by agency (Doom is evil and T'Challa is noble) or structure (wealth accumulation or unequal distribution are the necessary result to a process of inherent domination)? If we assume all wealth to be structurally bad, then we cannot explain rich superheroes like T'Challa, Bruce Wayne, Reed Richards (Mr. Fantastic), or Tony Stark.

Finally, inequality raises a moral question in international relations about the nature of globalization, of capitalism, and—ultimately—of human nature. Values such as equality, fraternity, inclusion, and solidarity (Pope Francis, 2015) are not economic interests or political ideas. They are not descriptive inquiries but normative imperatives. Here it is not about how globalization is, but about how it should be. Does the insurmountable gap in income distribution imply making choices in favor of accumulation at the expense of environmental degradation, social cohesion, or even cultural destruction? The financialization of the economy deepens inequality by generating a growing disconnect between Wall Street and Main Street. Ozymandias has in Veidt Enterprises a billion-dollar international conglomerate of companies that range from garments to perfumes, electronics, toys, and entertainment. Wayne Enterprises (of Batman) has equivalent reach and diversification. Should market values be applied to all aspects of social life? Applying Schumpeterian "creative destruction" on a global scale leads in practice not to general welfare but to negative eugenic economic extermination. Thanos proposes such a draconian solution in *Avengers: Infinity War*: by halving the

Universe´s population, he seeks to reduce the supply of people to balance the demand for food. In a mad Malthusian dialogue, Thanos explained to Dr. Strange:

Thanos: Too many mouths, not enough to go around. And when we faced extinction, I offered a solution.

Dr. Strange: Genocide?

Thanos: But at random, dispassionate, fair to rich and poor alike.

Chapter Thirteen

The X-Men

Migrants and Refugees

Migration has become in recent years a critical issue in both national and international politics. It has become a pressing theoretical and public policy concern. There are two main ways for understanding this from an international political economy perspective. *Pull* factors encourage or regulate migration to a receiving country: growth, wage differential, better living standards. *Push* factors drive people out of their home countries: environmental catastrophe, conflict and the ensuing displacement, human rights violations, economic crisis, or political persecution. Each factor creates relatively different subjects: migrants and refugees.

In 1970, the number of international labor migrants was 78 million. By 1990, it had almost doubled to more than 153 million. According to the UN's 2020 *World Migration Report*, the number of international migrants worldwide reached 281 million in 2020. Despite the growth of political restrictive measures in major destination countries, the growth of global migration shows no signs of slowing down. International migrants represent 3.6 percent of the world population, up from 2.8 percent in 2000. One-third of all international migrants come from just ten countries. India is the main country of origin of some 18 million people living abroad. Migrants from Mexico constituted the second-largest "diaspora" (12 million), followed by China (11 million), the Russian Federation (10 million), and the Syrian Arab Republic (8 million). Relatedly, the top three remittance recipients were India (US$78.6 billion), China (US$67.4 billion), and Mexico (US$35.7 billion). The growth of international labor migration in the era of globalization is remarkable, but still 95 percent of the world's population never leaves its country of origin. Although absolute flows of migrants have grown, they also remain a small minority. The vast majority of people continue to live in the countries in which they were born: only one in thirty are migrants.

Superman, for example, is an immigrant—and more than that, an illegal immigrant. As you can always count on good old Kal-El, he adopts to his core the nation that adopted him and puts his powers at the service of the American Way. He is male, white, polite, and honest and has relatively simple powers. The X-Men however are something different. They are not a team of superheroes (like the Avengers or the Fantastic Four) who save the world but wayward children who Professor Charles Xavier brings into the School for Gifted Youngsters (later Xavier Institute for Higher Learning) to teach them how to control their powers and learn how to use their budding superhuman abilities. They do not fit into the human world because they are mutants. They are considered weird, "freaks" . . . like refugees. The UN Refugee Agency's (UNHCR) December 2020 *Global Trends Report* estimated 82.4 million forcibly displaced people worldwide as a result of persecution, conflict, violence, human rights violations, or events seriously disturbing public order. Of these, 48.0 million are internally displaced people and 26.4 million refugees. Global asylum-seekers are 4.1 million, more than the population of Venezuela (3.9 million). An estimated 35 million (42 percent) of the 82.4 million forcibly displaced people are children below eighteen years of age, six hundred times the number of daily visitors to Disney World. There are also 4.2 million stateless people residing in ninety-four countries. More than two-thirds (68 percent) of all refugees abroad come from just five countries (as of the end of 2020): Syrian Arab Republic, Venezuela, Afghanistan, South Sudan, and Myanmar. Developing countries host 86 percent of the world's refugees. Turkey hosts the largest number of refugees (3.7 million), followed by Colombia, Pakistan, Uganda, and Germany. One person is forcibly displaced approximately every two seconds (37,000 per day).

The X-Men were the first Marvel superheroes whose power did not come from an accident or a military experiment. Mutants' powers are constitutive of their identity. That is why they operate like a "shadow" of globalization. According to Jung (1959), the idea of persona is "what oneself as well as others thinks one is." While the persona relates to the external world, the "shadow is that hidden, repressed, for the most part inferior and guilt-laden personality whose ultimate ramifications reach back into the realm of our animal ancestors. . . . If it has been believed hitherto that the human shadow was the source of evil, it can now be ascertained on closer investigation that the unconscious man, that is his shadow does not consist only of morally reprehensible tendencies, but also displays a number of good qualities, such as normal instincts, appropriate reactions, realistic insights or creative impulses." The individual shadow contains all the formless, underdeveloped, unwanted, and disowned psychological content that forms the individual unconscious. There is also a culturally determined collective unconscious that consists of that which opposes conscious, shared, and collective values. From infancy, humans learn what is acceptable and upheld or unacceptable and taboo. We repress what is unacceptable and in the process internalize our carers' attitudes toward unwanted qualities and characteristics of ourselves. The harsher the attitude, the more hostile we are to these facets of our shadow. And shadow can only be known through projecting it onto other individuals or groups (scapegoating). When William Stryker discovers that his son Jason is a mutant, he considers it a disease that needs to be cured. The colonel is encouraged to embrace the mutation of Jason by Professor Xavier. Enraged, he withdraws his son from Xavier's school. Jason becomes increasingly angry. Resentful and vengeful toward his parents, he blames them for his condition and begins to use his powers to torment them by planting illusions and horrible images in their minds. After his wife commits suicide trying to calm the visions, Stryker subjects his son to a forced lobotomy and keeps him cryogenically frozen. Unable to cope with his wife's death, he vows to eliminate all mutant humanity. This X-Men narrative is analogous to the problem between the European Union and those who cross the Mediterranean from Africa or between Mexican migrants and the United States. Magneto has experienced this firsthand. When he claims, "Mankind has always feared what it doesn't understand," he is talking both about the coming human-mutant war and the war he lived through as a boy, a victim of Nazism's concentration camps. The very existence of both the X-Men and migrants and refugees tests the values of a society by making it look in the mirror. Economically, migrants are workers (impact wages, income distribution, and investment priorities), students (increase the stock of human capital and diffusion of knowledge), entrepreneurs (create job opportunities and promote innovation and technological change), consumers (increase demand for goods and services and thus price and production levels), savers (send remittances to countries of origin bolstering the bank system), and taxpayers (contribute to the public budget and benefit from public services). But there is also a cultural and political side to the argument. Migrants or refugees are also family members who support their own. They create "co-ethnic networks" (Fitzgerald et al., 2014, p. 410), relocating to destinations where they can make use of connections. As the typical migrant is relatively less educated than the host population and does not have specialized skills, networks are key to minimizing risk and maximizing opportunities in destination countries. They may apply their family connections to obtain citizenship or permanent residence status. Migrants often come from the same area of origin (Galicians in Buenos Aires, Sicilians in New York, Okinawans in Peru) and thus create communities in their host countries (Little Italy, Chinatown, shtetls, Quartier Asiatique). Just like the X-Men, migrants question the established order and national identity by the mere fact of existing. They awaken passions not related to the real effects that the economic or political presence of foreigners has on the host society. As Gladys Pierpauli (2011) masterfully summarized: "There are two types of immigration: wanted and unwanted. The desired one is that in which governments assume to open their borders to include immigrants within the territorial, economic, political and cultural system. And the unwanted one, which is a side effect of the actions that the central countries do not want to see, the reverse of colonialism. This produces two visions: one in which migrants are presented as a destabilizing subject, alien, with an atavistic culture, with another skin color, another religion. The other is supportive and inclusive betting that through inclusion they will improve on existing conditions." Some argue foreign influences damage an ethos that host societies are quick to defend but not to define. In the *X-Men* film (2000), Senator Kelly has a list of names of identified mutants in the United States. During the hearing, he harangues one of the teachers of Xavier's school: "And there are even rumors, Miss Grey, of mutants so powerful that they can enter our minds and control our thoughts, taking away our God-given free will. Now I think the American people deserve the right to decide if they want their children to be in school with mutants. To be taught by mutants! Ladies and gentlemen, the truth is that mutants are very real, and that they are among us. We must know who they are, and above all, what they can do!" Nayak (2015) argues that the host country assesses the "value" of asylum seekers under a "dignified victim" mental framework with the host country being more "civilized." To Huntington (2004), the idea of the "melting pot" meant migrants left behind old identities and completely embraced new social customs, rights, and political obligations. The resulting national identity would be unified, though not homogeneous. Magneto represents the greatest fear of migrants: they will completely undermine or transform the foundations of the receiving country. Magneto is a mutant Malcolm X. When Malcolm Little chose "X" as his surname, he did so to symbolize the names stolen from African Americans when they were forced into slavery. Magneto forms the Brotherhood of Mutants, a group dedicated to the cause of mutant superiority over humans with an agenda toward either subjugating the human race to the will of mutants or eradicating humanity altogether. Magneto and Malcolm both reject the integration model proposed by Xavier and Martin Luther King. For them, integrating mutants/African Americans into the human/white society would destroy their identity, inhibiting true social and political equality. They both believe what Malcolm X declared in 1965: that there would "ultimately be a clash between the oppressed and those that do the oppressing, between those who want freedom, justice and equality for everyone and those who want to continue the systems of exploitation."

Chapter Fourteen

Climate Change

Aquaman in the Anthropocene

Arthur Curry is half human and half Atlantean, son of Queen Atlanna and lighthouse keeper Tom Curry. When Arthur's mother returned to Atlantis, Tom was forced to raise his son alone. Aquaman is a modern version of the Greek sea god Poseidon, even including a trident. In addition to superhuman strength, exceptional swimming ability, and control over sea life, he can breathe underwater and has telepathic abilities. Of all superheroes, Aquaman is probably the kindest: his powers are not destructive; he is a guardian of nature and a friend of the environment. Atlantis is an underwater kingdom that declares war on the surface world. The sovereign of the seas wants to stop the conflict peacefully but discovers that his own half-brother Orm is leading the warring faction (during the *Throne of Atlantis* crossover story-line, it was a plan of the Queen's royal counselor, Vulko). "Son of the Earth, King of the Seas": Aquaman himself experiences a conflict of loyalties between the underwater and surface worlds, between the Justice League and Atlantis. This conflict symbolizes the one the world faces today between economic growth and environmental care. Is there a "balance" between production and conservation? Is it philosophically possible to define it? Is it materially feasible for humanity to achieve it?

For Karl Marx (1976), capitalism causes a "metabolic failure" by the constant expansion of productivity. It disturbs the natural interaction between man and the earth because it prevents the return to the soil of its constituent elements consumed by man, thus hindering the functioning of the eternal natural condition. Industry replaces nature. The speed, scope, and scale of human industrial activities are having unparalleled, unintended, and poorly understood impacts on the earth as a system. Human impact on the ecosystem has become comparable to major geological events of the past. Human activities on a planetary scale are profoundly entangled with biological, ecological, geographical, and geological processes, leaving traces that will persist millions of years. Examples include habitat destruction and the introduction of invasive species, causing widespread extinctions; ocean acidification, changing the chemical composition of the seas; increase in erosion and sediment transport associated with urbanization and agriculture; global warming; sea-level rise; and global dispersion of many new "minerals" and "rocks," including concrete, fly ash, and plastics. Many of these changes are altering the trajectory of the Earth system, some with permanent effect reflected in a distinct body of geological strata now accumulating. So great is the impact that scientists are about to formally define a new geological unit within the Geological Time Scale: the Anthropocene.[21] The term—coined by Paul Crutzen and Eugene Stoermer in 2000—denotes the present geological time interval in which conditions and processes on Earth are profoundly altered by human impact. There is no doubt among scientists that human action is the main driver of global climate change. Regular temperatures, freshwater availability, and planetary biogeochemical flows are altered with results estimated to be irreversible.[22] If human activities push the Earth's biophysical systems out of stable equilibrium, the harmful or even catastrophic consequences will impede human development (Steffen et al., 2005). Authors such as Rockström (2009) propose "planetary boundaries" to define a safe operating space for humanity with respect to the Earth's natural system. The global ecosystem is difficult to predict because of the interaction of its many parts. Many of its component subsystems behave in nonlinear and often abrupt ways. They are particularly sensitive around threshold levels of certain key variables. If these thresholds are crossed, the consequences are potentially disastrous (Lenton et al., 2008). This is anthropomorphized when Atlantean king Orm decides to return the plastic and other pollutants that humans have been dumping into the ocean for centuries.[23] He creates tsunamis that crash across the planet, depositing mountains of waste on the world's beaches. Orm declares war on "the surface world" for destroying his marine home by polluting and overfishing it. Humans polluted nature; now it is returned to them as "green"—or more appropriately "blue"—justice. On key environmental issues such as pollution, climate change, natural resources, and population, objectives such as economic growth, human rights, and environmental protection come into conflict. They are integrally related and have transnational implications with nonlinear composite effects. Political decisions to address environmental issues are costly and can have unintended consequences. The environment is a global public good. All states benefit, but none can appropriate it exclusively. Preserving public goods depends on overcoming conflicting individual interests. The costs of damaging the environment are spread both across distances and through time. However, the benefits of environmentally unsustainable resource consumption are concentrated and can be appropriated by states, corporations, or private individuals. One example is carbon emission reduction targets: each country thinks its actions do not make a difference and that their failure to comply will not affect the final outcome. As no one nation fulfills its commitments, the aggregate result is emission increase and furthering the Earth's ozone layer depletion. Individually, there is no incentive to maintain public goods because they require commitments, agreements, and rules that transcend national borders. On June 2021, legal experts from across the globe unveiled a historic definition of *ecocide*—"unlawful or wanton acts committed with knowledge that there is a substantial likelihood of severe and widespread or long-term damage to the environment being caused by those acts"—intended to be adopted by the International Criminal Court to prosecute crimes against the environment. If adopted, it would become the fifth offense the court prosecutes, together with war crimes, crimes against humanity, genocide, and the crime of aggression. In line with the environment being a growing issue in international relations, it would also be the first new international crime since the 1940s.

Disruptions ranging from extreme weather events to large-scale changes in ecosystems are occurring at a pace and intensity unlike any other known period of time. Anthropogenic climate change is having an increasingly decisive impact on migration: millions around the world move in anticipation of or as a response to environmental stress every year: between 2008 and 2020, 89 percent of natural disasters were weather related (floods, storms, wildfires, and droughts) as opposed to the 11 percent geophysical (earthquakes or volcano eruptions). In 2018, the Philippines and China (approximately 3.8 million each), as well as India and the United States (respectively around 2.7 and 1.2 million), had the highest absolute numbers of large-scale displacement triggered by climate and weather-related hazards. Storms and floods alone were responsible for 98 percent of all disaster displacements in 2020. Cyclone Amphan alone triggered 5 million displacements across Bangladesh, Bhutan, India, and Myanmar. The Atlantic hurricane season was the most active on record with thirty named storms, including hurricanes Iota and Eta, which affected twelve Central American and Caribbean countries. At least 7 million people were internally displaced by natural disasters across 104 countries and territories as of December 31, 2020. The World Bank estimates by 2050 the number of climate refugees could reach 143 million. The interaction between climate, armed conflict, and poverty increases the complexity of issues such as migration and terrorism. For example, worsening droughts in Somalia coupled with Shabab-related violence are driving thousands of people to flee within the country or to travel to Ethiopia. As we saw with the X-Men, displacement itself is often a source of tension and conflict. Add to this the adverse effects of climate change, and competition for natural resources, land, food, and water intensifies.

In Aquaman's world, environmental conflict gets entangled in political dispute in the very same way it is happening in the real world today. The "environmental war" between humans and Atlanteans is at the same time defined by the succession dispute between Orm and Arthur. In times of power transition, geopolitical tensions, and geoeconomic dislocation, the increasingly competitive world scene is disintegrating the necessary global cooperation to reach a planetary multilateral environmental agreement. The Paris Agreement is a legally binding international treaty on climate change adopted by 196 parties that entered into force on November 2016. Its goal is to limit global warming to well below 2, preferably 1.5 degrees Celsius, compared to preindustrial levels. To achieve this long-term temperature goal, countries commit themselves to reach global peaking of greenhouse gas emissions as soon as possible to achieve a climate-neutral world by mid-century. This agreement assumes the persistence of international economic and political conditions. And it does not take into account domestic policy pressures in each of the party states. Worldwide, national governments find themselves increasingly polarized and paralyzed in the face of the greatest global threat facing humanity.

Environmental issues demand new frameworks of thought and action for international relations. It is imperative to understand the multiple and interrelated issues (poverty, energy, climate, population, infrastructure, security, economy) and the existing governance structures at various levels (local, subnational, national, international, transnational). Sustainability—the notion that basic ecological conditions must be maintained so that the ability of future generations to meet their needs is not compromised—is increasingly a part of international affairs. The infinite supply of space and resources formed Adam Smith's economic idea of capitalist development in the eighteenth century. In our current twenty-first century, planetary limits are becoming harshly evident. Ecological issues have become one of the main ideological battlefields of today. A first set of arguments dismisses the issue as marginal phenomena, not worthy of the investment of political resources since nature naturally regenerates itself. The next set of arguments are those of the utopians that bet on humanity's technocratic tradition to adapt by building ourselves out of troublesome situations. Technology (geoengineering, deliberate tampering of the Earth's climate via processes like launching sulfur dioxide into the stratosphere to create a haze against sun radiation that would cool the world) or the market (taxes, carbon credits) will provide a solution. And if that fails, they dream about life on other planets. A third line of argument is more psychological and emphasizes personal moral responsibility rather than large systemic measures. Greta Thunberg personifies this view: a sixteen-year-old child with a powerful voice carrying an unflinching message, delivered with "righteous rage and eyes glistening with hope and determination," as Frank Miller described her in DC's *Dark Knight Returns: The Golden Child #1* (2019). Many have come to believe this is the best hope for progress on climate action. A final one is to herald a return to "natural balance" or doom humanity to a dystopian future of capitalism-induced environmental catastrophe. The world should pursue a more modest traditional life in tune not with enlightened "arrogance" but with the "humility" of being children of "Mother Earth."[24] On November 28, 2008, president of Bolivia Evo Morales, issued a public letter titled "Climate Change: Save the Planet from Capitalism." The opening paragraph read: "Sisters and brothers: Today, our Mother Earth is ill. . . . Everything began with the industrial revolution in 1750, which gave birth to the capitalist system. In two and a half centuries, the so-called developed countries have consumed a large part of the fossil fuels created over five million centuries. Under capitalism Mother Earth does not exist, instead there are raw materials. Capitalism is the source of the asymmetries and imbalances in the world."

Marvel superheroes were children of the atomic age, and thus science played a central role in granting them powers (Spider-Man's radioactive spider, Hulk's gamma rays, the experimental space flight that exposed the Fantastic Four to cosmic rays). We are now in an environmental era that will gradually (re)define superhero narratives. Instead of being admired for their superhuman abilities, caped heroes are being assessed on bases such as their attitudes toward planets and their ecosystems, how much the superhero's natural ability could harm the planet, what kind of weapon(s) the superhero wields and how it impacts the environment, or if his or her choice of transportation wastes energy and fuel or has a greener means of travel. A global sustainability-centered perspective brings to the fore a focus on collective survival and well-being. For international relations, it moves understanding away from a state-centered view fixated on traditional notions of power and sovereignty and into new forms of governance through cultural changes and the spread of ecological awareness. It argues that it is possible, desirable, and even necessary to maintain air, water, and land quality. It promotes new sources and criteria for legitimacy and cements a sense of intergenerational responsibility. If the impending ecological crisis threatens civilization or survival of the human species, it is imperative to explore a sustainable world order. Can we imagine, define, advance, and defend a radical reconceptualization of world affairs under a global environmental conceptual basis? This will surely be a task for future sustainable superheroes, forging and fostering a new era of global *ecopolitics*.

Chapter Fifteen

Green Lantern

Battlefield Space

Billions of years ago, natives of the overpopulated planet Maltus[25] evolved into a race of immortals with powerful mental abilities. One member of their race, a scientist named Krona, looked into the past to learn the origin of creation. In doing so, he accidentally unleashed a wave of energy that split the universe into a Multiverse. It also created the evil Anti-Matter Universe. Guilt-ridden, a group left and settled on the planet Oa, located in the center of the universe. There they cast off their emotions and became Guardians of the Universe: the Green Lantern Corps. Each Lantern has a power ring of advanced technology that allows the bearer to project green energy rays and make hard-light constructs of any size or shape.

Today, space is an area of international relations fast becoming a decisive realm for power competition. Space weaponization is not a new phenomenon. Militarization has been a controversial issue for decades. But a large number of technological developments have led to a drastic acceleration in the destructive potential of space warfare and are rapidly transforming outer space into a new domain of war on a par with water (surface and underwater), land, air, and cyberspace. The UN Committee on the Peaceful Uses of Outer Space dates from 1957 and established international outer space law. The 1967 Outer Space Treaty forbids placing "nuclear weapons or other weapons of mass destruction in orbit or on celestial bodies." In addition, states are not allowed to establish military stations or conduct military maneuvers on the moon or other planetary objects. What the treaty does not cover, however, is the definition of *peaceful*, the transit of nuclear weapons *through* space, the placement of *conventional* weapons in space, and the launch of nuclear weapons from Earth into space. Here we find our first

superhero explanatory symmetry: Green Lantern is not an individual superhero but a member of an intergalactic soldier force. Keeping outer space as a
global common is critical to global peace and security.

The Green Lantern Corps currently has 7,200 members, two for each
space sector.[26] The Union of Concerned Scientists (UCS) Satellite Database
counted 3,372 operating satellites as of January 2021. Of these, 1,897 are
American (34 civilian, 1,486 commercial, 165 governmental, and a further
212 exclusively military), 176 Russian, 412 Chinese, and 887 of other na-
tionalities. Using space for military purposes (such as using satellites to
guide the military or collect intelligence) is different from the physical placing of weapons in space to target locations or objects on Earth and in space.
However, most space technology has multiple purposes, and there is no
universally agreed-upon definition of what space weapons are. As "force-
multipliers," satellites are already part of warfare operations. While they do
not execute actual combat operations on their own, they are used to guide
ground forces and provide detailed intelligence information on potential targets. In 2001, the US military relied on satellites for enhanced precision
weaponry in Afghanistan. Corporate satellites far outnumber government
and military satellites, reflecting a growing trend for the private sector to
become more involved in space technology. For-profit development efforts
include space mining operations and programs that allow tourists to pay to
experience a journey beyond the Earth's atmosphere. This has helped in the
diffusion of satellite technology to emerging countries without their own
space programs. For example, Luxembourg operates more active satellites
than large European countries such as Germany, Spain, and Italy. The monarchy recently launched the Luxembourg Space Agency (LSA), which commercialized its launch capabilities. There is a growing number of private
companies offering satellite launch capabilities to private customers and national governments, leading to a growing interdependence of interests between industry and governments in the militarization of space. In 2020, civil
budgets totaled US$50.2 billion, 61 percent of total spending. This was sup-
ported by more emerging players investing, more ambitious civil programs
by great powers in exploration and crewed spaceflight, and a growing commercial market. Global revenue from space-based services annually exceeds
$300 billion, more than two-thirds in the commercial sector. Well over $100
billion in annual revenues arises from commercial space data services (mostly direct-to-home television). Over $100 billion derives from commercial
space equipment manufacturing. Defense space program budgets are driven
by a strong emphasis on space security in all leading space nations, a marked
interest in space situational awareness (SSA) by leading and emerging space
countries, and a generalized trend toward the militarization of space.

There are White, Orange, Red, Black, and Blue Lantern Corps. A number
of leading countries have been establishing space-focused defense organiza-

tions over the past five years, including the Russian Space Forces (2015), China's People's Liberation Army Strategic Support Force (2015), the US Space Force (2019), India's Defence Space Agency (2019), and Japan's Space Operation Squadron (2020). The United States remains the undisputed leader in government space spending, accounting for 58 percent of the world total ($47.7 billion in 2020). As countries start to consider the American space weaponization program threatening, they will take steps to defend themselves: a "space security dilemma" (Green Lantern meets Tony Stark). In 2020, China consolidated its second-place position at $8.9 billion. France—the highest European national spending—surged ahead to third place ($4 billion), driven by increasing European Space Agency (ESA) contributions and defense spending. Russia slid to fourth place as its public finance situation forced the country to reduce its space budget. Japan remained steady over the decade at around $3.3 billion. Space is increasingly deemed a warfighting domain by militaries around the world and increasingly included in defense policies. As geopolitical tensions rise across the world, so does the importance of space as a competitive and strategic edge. Countries with comprehensive space programs possess distinct military, economic, and scientific advantages. Traditional military space powers still drive initiatives and investments (United States, Japan, Russia, China, and France), but new players are increasing investments (European Union, India, United Arab Emirates, Australia). Unlike the Lantern Corps, complexity, expense, and barriers to entry have allowed only a few "space nations" to develop capabilities. While only eleven nations now have the space industrial capacity to develop, manufacture, launch, and operate their own space systems, more than fifty have purchased and operate satellites and have partial elements of a space industrial base.

Great powers are increasing the development of military space capabilities. Most defense experts consider space to be the ultimate military high ground. In March 2019, India became the fourth country (after the United States, Russia, and China) to test an anti-satellite weapon (ASAT). The realm of space weapons is like Hal Jordan's ring: only limited by imagination and willpower. Hypersonic weapons have transformed kinetic attacks (direct strikes such as missiles, defense batteries, or detonation of a warhead near a satellite or Earth satellite station). They fly at speeds of at least Mach 5 (five times the speed of sound). There are two categories of hypersonic weapons: hypersonic glide vehicles (launched from a rocket before gliding to a target) and hypersonic cruise missiles (powered by high-speed engines). Hypersonic weapons do not follow a ballistic trajectory and can maneuver en route to their target. There is currently no defense against hypersonic weapons. Hypersonic missiles rely on satellites to function properly, and for this reason, both Russia and China are increasingly developing the capacity to disrupt (through electronic attacks that interfere with space data transmission systems) or destroy US satellites. This could render the US military both blind and deaf, subsequently obscuring the precise targeting capabilities of hypersonic missiles for moving targets, which require a steady stream of data. Directed-energy weapons (colloquially referred to as "lasers") use concentrated electromagnetic energy, rather than kinetic energy, to incapacitate, damage, disable, or destroy enemy equipment, facilities, or personnel. High-powered microwave weapons and electromagnetic pulses have been tested as a nonkinetic means of disabling electronics and communications systems. Finally, quantum sensors could provide alternative positioning, navigation, and timing options that could in theory allow militaries to continue to operate at full performance in GPS-denied environments.

Paraphrasing the Green Lantern Corps oath: "in brightest day, in blackest night, nothing escapes space's sight," which is now a more competitive and contested domain of international relations. And also congested: more than sixty years of space activities have left large quantities of uncontrolled debris in orbital lanes. As of May 2021, NASA estimated 23,000 pieces of debris larger than a softball orbiting the Earth at speeds up to 17,500 mph, fast enough to damage a satellite or a spacecraft. There are half a million pieces of debris the size of a marble (up to 0.4 inches, or 1 centimeter) or larger and approximately 100 million pieces of debris about .04 inches (or one millimeter) and larger. Space junk weighs a combined total of 8,800 tons.[27] Any accident in space could set in motion a chain of events leading to space war, especially in a field with an increasing presence of AI entities and lethal autonomous weapon systems capable of independently identifying a target and employing onboard weapon systems to engage and destroy the target without manual human control.

Part IV

The Players

Global Superpowers and Subpowers

This final section is dedicated to the main actors in world affairs, great powers like the United States (Captain America), China (Fu Manchu), and Russia (Hulk). We also consider the European Union and its particular kind of power (Wonder Woman). Black Panther and Wakanda—which the World Trade Organization once featured in its trade databases—will help us explore the emerging world. Writing from Argentina, I have also added a chapter on Latin America with one of the most beloved comic characters south of the Rio Grande: Juan Salvo, the Eternaut.

Chapter Sixteen

The United States

Is Captain America Retiring?

Captain America is the symbol of America's role in the world since World War II. "Role in the world" in foreign policy terms generally refers to the overall character, purpose, and direction of a country's participation in international affairs or its overall relation to the rest of the world. The United States summarized its own role in four key elements: (a) exercising global leadership; (b) creating and defending the liberal international order; (c) promoting freedom, democracy, and human rights; and (d) preventing the emergence of hegemons that could establish regional spheres of influence, especially in Eurasia.[28] This role is now more than seventy-five years old; both the Cap and American hegemony are at retirement age. A critical theoretical and practical issue in current international relations is determining if the superpower of our time is in decline.

Global leadership means becoming the most important country to identify, frame, and respond to international problems. In his iconic 1941 debut cover, the Cap appeared punching Hitler in the face. Putting the Führer, a still-living world leader, on the cover of a comic book as the villain was as daring as it was dangerous.[29] At the time, there was a strong isolationist feeling in America and a not negligible number of Axis supporters. But the Captain *is* America: he embodies a normative view on international power. Only America could send its children from Iowa or Nebraska to fight and die in the trenches of France and Germany. Those Farm Belt, corn-fed, tall, and healthy GIs paraded admirable and proud through a war-torn, hunger-stricken Old Continent as demigods, saviors whose might was a reflection of their right. The Cap is not a mercenary; he is not even a regular Avenger. He is a superhero who starts a "civil war" rather than compromising his principles by signing the Sokovia Accords to monitor and regulate the Avengers. In the same way, the United States is not a normal country. The United States has been called leader of the free world, superpower, indispensable nation, hyperpower, world police, and global hegemon. Global leadership is going beyond sheer geopolitical calculations. The ability and willingness to occupy this extraordinary international place were critical to building the liberal international order in the years immediately following the Second World War. American foreign policy was described as internationalist, of global engagement, of liberal order building, liberal internationalism, liberal hegemony, and interventionist. The aim was to avoid falling back into the spiral of competition, economic crisis, and war of the first half of the twentieth century. The United States paid the political costs (by setting up binding institutions that could constrain the exercise of its power), economic costs (humanitarian aid, trade preferences), and human costs of maintaining the international order (626,319 military deaths up to March 2020, 18 in the year since Memorial Day 2020, and just 3 deaths as of May 27, 2021). This order prioritized America´s political objectives, promoted its economic interests, and underpinned its global primacy. But the content of this order includes elements attractive to all: respect for territorial integrity, a preference for settling disputes peacefully and in accordance with international law, and an open trade system—limited and imperfect but preferable to one based on power alone, in which the most powerful countries impose their will unconstrained by rules, even if their application is at times hypocritical. The third element is the defense of freedom, democracy, and human rights as universal values. This is perhaps the most controversial point, since this defense was an instrument of US soft power and has not always been respected (between 1919 and 2020 there is documentary evidence of 349 instances of America's use of force abroad, including military and clandestine operations). Steve Rogers is also Captain *America* (as in *United States*). And although he appears to be fighting for all mankind, he wears the American colors on his uniform and shield. The last element reflects American geopolitics. A large enough concentration of regional power could threaten the vital interests cf the United States (Russia in Eurasia, Germany in Europe, Japan/China in Asia). In the pursuit of this fourth objective, Washington supported regimes that were in direct collision with the third objective.

A change in the US role would have significant and even profound effects on global security, freedom, and prosperity. Some argue the United States has substantially changed its role in the world, assuming a more restricted position as a result of changing global (relative decline owing to the rise of the emerging countries and China's growth) and domestic circumstances (absolute decline owing to debt, deficit, political paralysis, social polarization, and—some argue—moral decline). Cap also started completely selfless, jumping on grenades willy-nilly, and slowly became more self-interested.

Not selfish, but civil war shows him making decisions based on what he wants, even if it means breaking up the Avengers: *Captain America First*. A more circumscribed role reducing US involvement in world affairs would be tantamount to voluntary retirement. But what would a new US role look like? It could involve a voluntary retreat from or abdication of global leadership, greater reliance on unilateralism, reduced willingness to work through international or multilateral institutions and agreements, acceptance of US isolation or near-isolation on certain international issues, a more skeptical view of the value of alliances to the United States, a less-critical view of certain authoritarian or illiberal governments, a reduced or more selective approach to promoting and defending certain universal values, elevation of bilateral trade balances, commercial considerations, monetary transactions, ownership of strategic assets such as oil above other foreign policy considerations, and tolerance of the reemergence of aspects of global power politics instead of a reassertion of the principles of the international liberal order.

Can we—as Falcon asks—live in a world without Captain America? Of course, this question can only be asked in America. The agony over US decline seems more the anxiety of a superpower that—as the tango goes—"is no longer" than a fact-based conclusion. However, even if we can agree that America is not indispensable, that does not mean it is not necessary. What would happen to international relations in the absence of US primacy? Who has the will or the skill? When Rogers retires to live in peace with Peggy Carter, his shield and identity are passed to his friend Sam Wilson. This is an easy transition, for Falcon shares all of Cap's interests and values, the same commitment, and the ability to uphold his standards. Moreover, they are both united under an "institutional" structure of belonging to the Avengers. What would a non-US order look like? Would the world be doomed to (dis)order? What new power or combinations of powers could fill the vacuum? The actors that are filling Cap's void are China, Russia, and regional powers such as France, Germany, Turkey, and Iran. These and other powers have their own ideas about the international order, ideas that do not always coincide with the current liberal order. A renegotiated international order would mean different ideas and values on issues such as democracy, human rights, rule of law, free trade, autonomy of civil society, freedom of expression, association and information, individual rights, and state authority. The changing global distribution of power and wealth is gradually unfavorable for Washington. It is increasingly challenging and costly to afford global leadership without ideas from China and other countries. Collisions will be more frequent, concessions more difficult. Thus, in current world affairs, Captain America is not passing down his shield to someone who will try his best to fill in. America faces reluctant allies, undependable partners, incapable friends, and downright foes interested in destroying his legacy. Some want to change the shield's colors and logo; others question whether there should be a shield, still others the mechanism for selecting the bearer—and some even the very existence of superheroes.

Chapter Seventeen

Wonder Woman

The EU's Soft Power

At the end of the Second World War, Europe was geographically divided. A menacing Soviet Union stood at the border of the Western liberal democratic world. Europe turned to the United States for defensive security. Throughout the Cold War, Europe's security was essentially defined in political and military terms: the avoidance of direct military confrontation or indirect political infiltration. The continent's security was deemed to hinge on maintaining a (nuclear) balance of power between Washington and Moscow. So European security policy was forged under American protection within the framework of the North Atlantic Treaty Organization (NATO). In the following decades, countries gradually integrated to overcome the legacy of power politics that had brought devastation to all: security based on interdependence and shared sovereignty under regional institutions. Europe's lack of will to have offensive power came from the early integration by the European Coal and Steel Community. The ECSC interconnected the coal and steel manufacturing sectors in Germany, France, Italy, and the Benelux Union. The response was twofold: as long as key sectors of the German economy were interconnected with other European nations, the incentives for domination on the continent would diminish. The same reasoning applies to the theory of interdependence of the JLA, of which Diana Prince is a member. America's global leadership guaranteed Europe's security and enabled it to enjoy the peace dividend and imagine its role in the world "without" power, strategy, or geopolitics. The end of the Cold War produced a drastic change in the global and regional security environment. The collapse of the Soviet Union ended the possibility of war, removing the main security threat. The European Economic Community (EEC) had evolved into the more comprehensive European Union (EU) in 1993. The EU Member States had long ceased being a threat to one another. An enlarged and deepened bloc extended to Central and Eastern Europe. Today the EU is a unique economic and political union between twenty-seven countries (on January 31, 2020, the United Kingdom left the European Union); it governs 448 million lives.

The EU was Washington's main partner in building a global order based on liberal institutions, democracy, and free markets. European integration has been closely linked to multilateralism and a rules-based international order. Europe saw itself as the model and the vanguard of the future of world affairs: a "civil power" (Duchêne, 1972), "post-modern state" (Cooper, 2000), "normative power" (Manners, 2006), and "of Venus" (Kagan, 2004).[30] All these denominations attempt to capture a qualitatively different essence of the EU: lack of military capabilities, intergovernmental decision-making process, voluntary cession of national sovereignty. In short, Europe would have a special predisposition to act in a "civil," "normative," or "post-modern" manner in world affairs. Today, it declares to hold the values of human dignity, freedom, democracy, equality, rule of law, and human rights. The values of peace, compassion, love, and truth are present as a part of Wonder Woman's iconic weaponry. The lasso of truth is virtually unbreakable and, partnered with Diana's speed and strength, able to subdue nearly any opponent. This symbolizes the epitome of a "normative power": ideational rather than material or physical and its application involves a normative justification rather than material incentives or physical force. The bracelets of submission deflect projectiles and blunt attacks. They represent the Amazon's freedom from oppression and a reminder never to be bound again, much like the EU is an attempt to break the cycle of mutual destruction that ravaged the continent until the mid-twentieth century. The Themysciran shield can deflect heavy weaponry. And the Golden Eagle armor provides protection against physical and energy attacks (gunfire, explosions, electric shocks). It has a pair of wings attached to it so that Diana can fly, making her look as celestial and majestic as normative power should. Indeed, in the 2020 *Wonder Woman 1984* film, Cheetah attempts to shred the armor, in a scene much reflective of the European security strategy. Diana keeps folding the armor inward while it gets dented and torn to pieces from the outside. Even in the midst of the battle, Wonder Woman attempts moral rehabilitation of her enemy: "Nothing good is born from lies, Barbara. We're wasting precious time." To which Cheetah (a non-normative power) replies, shocked and outraged: "Even now, patronizing me." As for hard or offensive power,[31] the God Killer sword is dismissed as "aggressive," ultimately revealed to be nothing but a trick that disintegrates. This highlights the EU's lack of preference for conventional military capabilities. Wonder Woman could use her royal tiara as a projectile (much like the British queen played a role against Nazism), and her plane is . . . well, invisible.

At a time of growing geopolitical tensions, the EU can no longer approach international economic relations as essentially mutually beneficial or cooperative. Russia's European character is more dubious today than at any time during the post–Cold War period. Moscow has not aspired to follow the European model for years and is now leaning heavily toward Beijing. Increasingly intense competition between the United States and China may divide the world into a new bipolarity, creating nonpermissive conditions for the EU's survival as members are forced to choose sides. A case in point is telecommunications. The current controversy over the role of Chinese firm Huawei in introducing fifth generation (5G) wireless technology in Europe is an early sign of how the EU may get caught up in the US–China rivalry. The United States has issued strong warnings that letting Huawei in could divert confidential data to China. In July 2020, Britain closed the door to the Chinese tech giant. Beijing in turn sent ominous messages about the negative consequences for European business interests if Huawei is excluded from this important market. China's growing power and ability to jeopardize US interests should make US officials more appreciative of European allies. And Europe has reaffirmed its position: historically close to the United States due to shared values. China—although an indispensable economic partner and global stakeholder—has a political system based on values that are very different from European ones. Transatlantic power relations resemble the Wonder Woman–Superman relationship.

It was journalist and feminist activist Gloria Steinem who was responsible for restoring Wonder Woman to her original role as an icon of power and strength. Wonder Woman from Zack Snyder's *Batman v. Superman* films: *Dawn of Justice* (2016) and *Justice League* (2017) take up the Steinem tradition. And it continues in Patty Jenkins's films (*Wonder Woman*, 2017, and *Wonder Woman 1984*, 2020). The character is strong and independent. She sees no gender difference, part of a point of equality between men and women. In the belief that the EU is reluctant to respond to their concerns, many EU members increasingly turn to partnerships with each other, with China, or with the United States. Subregional alignments are growing. In Central Europe, the Visegrad Group (V4) was founded in 1991, comprising Hungary, Slovakia, Poland, and the Czech Republic. The theme that united the V4 was the categorical rejection of fixed quotas for refugees. Eastern Europe has the Three Seas Initiative. In the East, the twelve EU nations located between the Baltic, Black, and Adriatic Seas (Austria, Bulgaria, Croatia, Czech Republic, Estonia, Hungary, Latvia, Lithuania, Poland, Romania, Slovakia, and Slovenia) are seeking greater cooperation in economic development and infrastructure, especially energy. Southern Europe (Italy, Greece, Spain) is increasingly seeking to resolve its financial constraints through an alternative route to the EU. The United Kingdom has resorted to leaving the Union altogether.

The EU as a bloc is in question today. Can there be a post-modern power in a modern or even pre-modern world? Can a normative power survive in a geopolitical world? Or will systemic pressures fracture the EU back into its component parts? Since 2000, the leadership of the United States has declined. The EU has *sovereignist* neighbors (Russia, Turkey), who emphasize the sovereignty of the state at the expense of respect for fundamental human rights and civil societies that demand more freedom. Add the return of Russia to power politics, the advance of China, and the departure of one of its members, and the EU is due for a new political project and security strategy to hold it together. By mid-2020, there were two main ideas in the EU Council to return the EU to a status of global power as Steinem did with her childhood heroine. The first, promoted by Germany, is the *Green Deal*, a plan to make the EU carbon neutral by 2050.[32] France is the promoter of the other: *L'Europe Geopolitique*. The creator of Wonder Woman, William Moulton Marston, said she "encourages women to stand up for themselves, to learn to fight, and be strong, so they don't have to be scared, or depend on men." Could that phrase be an inspiration for Brussels today? The encouraging message from Jenkins's vision of Wonder Woman's power can serve the EU: even in a harsh world, soft power (sensitivity and compassion) can disarm. Diana Prince comes across in the film as compassionate, emotional, argumentative, and sensitive while being intelligent and ambitious and fighting when necessary. She does not have to be hard, tough, and troubled to be strong. In the face of the murderous, backstabbing Cersei from *Game of Thrones* (Russia) or the ice-veined power player Claire Underwood from *House of Cards* (China), Diana Prince can present an alternative to a race to "out-evil" (blunt force, sheer power competition) each other.

Chapter Eighteen

Emerging Countries

Welcome to Wakanda

There is no globally accepted definition of emerging markets. Academics, international institutions, and investment houses have different perspectives on what constitutes an emerging market or emerging economy. Nor is there an established convention for designating "developed" and "developing" countries or areas in the United Nations system. In common practice, Japan in Asia, Canada and the United States in North America, Australia and New Zealand in Oceania, and Europe are considered "developed" regions or areas. In international trade statistics, the Southern African Customs Union and Israel are also treated as developed. Some subgroups are defined based either on geographical location or on ad hoc criteria, such as the subgroup of "major developed economies," which is based on the membership of the G7. "Developing economies" include primarily countries in Asia, Africa, Latin America, the Pacific, and the Caribbean, not including the transition countries of Europe. Countries emerging from the former Yugoslavia are treated as developing countries, and countries of Eastern Europe and the former USSR countries in Europe are not included under either developed or developing regions. The IMF uses three levels to differentiate between "advanced economies" and "emerging and developing economies"[33]: seven-year average per capita income, export diversification, and degree of integration into the global financial system. The World Bank considers emerging market and developing economies (EMDEs) according to their gross national income per capita.[34] And the World Trade Organization (WTO) does not have its own definition of "developed" or "developing" countries, leaving it to members to decide for themselves whether they consider themselves "developed" or "developing."[35] The term "developing" now refers to what was previously called the "Third World," a "non-industrialized nation," or an "underdeveloped" country. These terms were pejorative, ethnocentric, and (almost) racist, as they attributed lower levels of socioeconomic development to natural, ethnic, or religious factors. "Developing" maintains a condescending tone, by implicitly welcoming the "young promise" or "good student country." Still, it negates recognition as a full-fledged equal.

In the Marvel universe, Wakanda is an independent African nation ruled by King T'Challa (Black Panther). Ryan Coogler's film *Black Panther* (2018) places Wakanda somewhere around Rwanda. The country is bordered by "hills, mountains, and the sprawling Lake Nyanza." In the movie, it is also protected by a hologram that hides its capital city from outside eyes. The country is among the most technologically advanced in the world and one of the few places where the near-indestructible metal vibranium (the material of Captain America's shield) is found. Vibranium is capable of absorbing kinetic energy and releasing it later, and its almost inexhaustible supply has made Wakanda the most technologically advanced nation on Earth: it split the atom decades before the United States and has a cure for cancer. To protect its resources and inhabitants, it has cloaked itself by advanced technology and is secluded from the rest of the world. Wakanda passes as an impoverished ("least developed," international organizations would say) country that refuses to receive international aid. In reality it is a shrewd development strategy. The country did not fall into the *resource curse* (Auty, 1994; Sachs and Warner, 2001; Ross, 1999; Robinson et al., 2006). Resource abundance would seem to guarantee instant fortune, when it actually leads to conflict, corruption, and poverty. Revenue from extracting raw materials might be mismanaged or embezzled by government officials or siphoned off by foreign corporations. The bonanza might crowd out investment in other parts of the economy and make goods and services more expensive. History is full of countries—especially for smaller and less diverse economies—whose natural-resource wealth led to ruined economic growth, deteriorated governance, and degraded environment. Wakanda's dilemmas are similar to those faced by emerging and developing countries: (1) modern, technological sectors of the economy coexist with traditional barter and subsistence; (2) the stock of resource wealth is higher than the actual national prosperity; (3) the state has a preeminent role in economic and industrial development; (4) colonialism has made people distrustful of international relations and thus policies swing between isolation and integration to the world economy;[36] and (5) societies do not see themselves as part of a global liberal community but define their identity in strong cultural/tribal/ethnic/civilizational terms.[37]

Emerging countries symbolize three simultaneous transitions currently under way in different dimensions of the international system: economic, political, and cultural. In the past, advanced countries concentrated economic prosperity and dominated production. In 1990, the share of world output was

63 percent for the advanced and 37 percent for the emerging countries. That had been the historical standard of capitalism but is no longer the case. Since the early 2000s, the trend has reversed. In 2001, the proportion was 57 percent to 43 percent. By 2007, it had reached 50–50 parity; in 2017, it was 41 percent for advanced and 59 percent in favor of emerging countries. In 2021, the IMF estimated 41–58 percent, reaching 40–60 percent in 2024. Moreover, emerging countries constitute the main drivers of global economic growth: they have contributed more than 80 percent of global growth since the financial crisis of 2008. Emerging economies are increasingly driving global consumption by shifting purchasing power from advanced countries to the growing middle classes in emerging countries. Between 2020 and 2040, 75 percent of the global GDP growth will come from emerging and developing markets, bringing up their share in the global economy in purchasing power parity (PPP) terms to 69 percent. The second transition is taking place because emerging countries are seeking to translate their economic importance into *political* influence. The G7 (Canada, France, Germany, Italy, Japan, the United Kingdom, and the United States) seems increasingly outdated as the world's executive committee and has given way in practice to the G20[38] as the most representative body of actual distribution of international power. The same is true for global governance institutions such as IMF and the World Bank. The Netherlands and Belgium together have the same voting power as China, although they represent only 1.68 percent of the world economy and China 16 percent, ten times more. Germany (the most powerful country in Europe) and Japan are not on the UN Security Council. Neither are countries like Brazil or India. Like Erik Killmonger declares to the Wakandan Council: "The world's gonna start over and this time we're on top." Finally, emerging countries are culturally different. Geert Hofstede (2011) defines culture as "the collective programming of the mind distinguishing the members of one group or category of people from others." For almost two hundred years, since the mid-nineteenth century, international affairs were dominated by middle-aged white Christian (mostly Protestant) men from the upper-middle class. Hofstede offers six cultural dimensions that represent independent preferences for one state of affairs over another that distinguish countries (rather than individuals) from each other. For example, *power distance* expresses the degree to which the less powerful members of a society accept and expect that power is distributed unequally. Wakanda is a theocratic (the leader of the Panther tribe was visited by the panther god Bast, who instructed him to drink the Heart-Shaped Herb to acquire superpowers) monarchy (although entitled to challenge, T'Challa inherited rule from his father T'Chaka). In other Hofstedean dimensions critical for the coming international order issues, emerging countries also differ. Advanced countries score more on individualism (preference for a loosely knit social framework in which individuals are expected to take care of only themselves and their

immediate families) and emerging countries on collectivism (preference for a tightly knit framework in society in which individuals can expect their relatives or members of a particular ingroup to look after them in exchange for unquestioning loyalty). This replicates over uncertainty avoidance, or long-term orientation versus short-term normative orientation, or indulgence versus restraint. When the mantle of global economic and political leadership passed from the United Kingdom to the United States, the power transition took place within a similar cultural (Anglo-Protestant), political (limited government), and economic (free market) framework. What will the future be like? India is the world's largest democracy and is not Western; Russia is a "competitive authoritarianism" (Levitsky and Way, 2002), "anocracy" (Vreeland, 2008), or "hybrid regime" (Diamond, 2002). And the Chinese regime has fused a capitalist production system with communist political governance in a system exhibiting growing elements of its imperial past. Without falling into cultural reductionism or essentialism, the rise of emerging countries discusses (will it also dispute?) the parameters with which the balance between public and private, state and market, authority and responsibility, rights and obligations, obedience and power is established. Wakanda forever?

Chapter Nineteen

China

From Fu Manchu to the Mandarin

China became the world's largest exporter of goods in 2009, the largest trading nation in 2013, the world's largest economy in terms of purchasing power parity (PPP) in 2014, the fifth-largest exporter of services in 2017, and the second-largest importer of services in the world in 2018. It is the main export destination for thirty-three countries and the largest source of imports for sixty-five. It is the locomotive of world growth. Between 1961 and 1978, China's average annual contribution to global economic growth was 1 percent. But from 1979 to 2012, it was 16 percent; from 2013 to 2018, 28 percent. China alone accounted for 24 percent of global energy consumption in 2019 and is the world's largest importer of oil and natural gas. China consumes 30 percent of the world's soybeans, 40 percent of cell phones, 45 percent of steel, and 50 percent of copper. One out of every two pigs in the world are Chinese. The country consumed between 2011 and 2013 more cement (6.6 gigatons) than the United States consumed throughout the twentieth century (4.5 gigatons from 1901 to 2000). Are these numbers enough to declare Chinese dominance of the twenty-first century?

Fu Manchu or "Dr." Fu Manchu is English writer Sax Rohmer's most famous creation. This Chinese criminal genius was the hero-villain of novels and short stories. He also appeared in silent and sound films, radio serials, and comic strips. A descendant of the Chinese imperial family, the sinister Fu Manchu hates the Western world and the white race. He personified the genre of the "yellow peril" mystery, which expressed Western fears of the expansion of Asian power and influence. In times of increasing strategic rivalry and bipolar confrontation, he is useful to explain the scaremongering, ethnocentrism, and racism of Western powers. Western representations of the

East are as misleading as they are pernicious. Edward Said's (1979) term *orientalism* described a structured set of concepts, assumptions, and discursive practices used to produce, interpret, and evaluate knowledge about non-European peoples. The deconstruction of texts helps us understand how they reflected and reinforced the imperialist project. Arab "control" of oil prices, Japanese "unfair". competition, and most recently Chinese currency "manipulation" implicitly assume civilizational or ethnic characteristics to explain international behavior. Even if imperialism has disappeared, mental constructs remain in academia, popular culture, and government policy. Since at least 2007, the idea that China exports "poisons" to the world through its defective products—medicines, baby milk powder, lead-painted toys[39]—has been spread regularly. The problem is that explanations are not based on the shortcomings of production or the lack of oversight. Fringe theories are informed by racist stereotypes derived from delusional narratives about Chinese malevolence and ruthless global designs. The clearest and most recent example was US president Donald Trump calling SARS-CoV-2 the "Chinese virus."[40]

To achieve his evil objective of world domination, Fu Manchu has at his disposal a wealth of resources, an army of his own, advanced technology, venoms of all kinds, and trained animal assassins. China's ambitions as a rising power can clash with those of the West. Competition for resources and political and military control are indeed genuine causes for concern. However, in almost any issue related to China, old fears and biases resurface. On a global level, fantasies about cruel Chinese international conspiracies are akin to the "devil doctor's" characteristics: mysterious malignancy, inexplicable hatred of Western whites, and desire for global supremacy. In the 2012 remake of *Red Dawn*, MGM studios changed the script's original enemy (China) to North Korean troops. Max Brooks's film adaptation of *World War Z* changed the material so that the zombie outbreak did not start in China. Arkansas Senator Tom Cotton tweeted on April 20, 2020: "Did you know Hollywood is in China's pocket? China funds US movies & studios are desperate for access to the Chinese market. That's why China is never the bad guy in movies. That's why they took Taiwan's flag off Maverick's jacket in Top Gun 2. Time for this to end." Domestically, fears of an insidious Chinese presence are encouraged, causing public opinion to swing hysterically. From March 2020 to May 2021, more than 6,600 racist incidents against Asians were reported. The "Chinese virus" framing of the COVID-19 pandemic resembled the nineteenth-century blaming of Asians for malaria, cholera, and leprosy. The 2021 rash of violence against Asian Americans prompted US president Joe Biden to sign into law the COVID-19 Hate Crimes Act.

Fu Manchu helps us disentangle perceptions from reality, fact from fiction. China indeed has a new position of economic importance and international political influence. Is China gaining ground in the global telecommunications market? Yes. The Chinese Huawei and ZTE control 28 percent and 9.6 percent of the market. In 1992, China had more influence capacity than the United States in 33 countries, while the United States retained an advantage in 160 countries; by 2020, Chinese influence capacity had surpassed the United States in 61 countries. In the 140 states where the United States was still ahead, its lead had shrunk. Does the Chinese model of state capitalism fuse corporate and government interests? Yes. Does that warrant close scrutiny of the dual implications for profit and security? Most certainly. Could this pose a threat to individual freedom? Yes. Can we then conclude there is a secret malice or a ruthless design for domination by Beijing? No. The Chinese Communist Party's vision seems to be inclining toward a partial, loose, and malleable hegemony (Rolland, 2020)—partial for accepting spheres of influence as opposed to an ambition to rule the entire world; loose because Beijing is not striving for direct or absolute control over foreign territories or governments; and malleable because countries included under Chinese hegemony do not seem to be strictly defined along geographic, cultural, or ideological lines.

In Shane Black's *Iron Man 3* (2013), Happy Hogan is hospitalized after an attack by a character conspicuously named "The Mandarin." Upon leaving the hospital where his friend is hospitalized, Tony Stark is asked when someone is going to kill the Mandarin (notice the question is not *stop* him). Redoubling the bet, Stark replies: "There's no politics here; it's just good old-fashioned revenge. There's no Pentagon. It's just you and me." This seems to be the trend in which US–China relations are heading, not just trade conflict or power competition. Friends cooperate, competitors are defeated . . . but enemies are eliminated. There is a fundamental incompatibility, an impossibility of coexistence. In reality, Rohmer's Fu Manchu is Conan Doyle's Moriarty. Even in *Iron Man*, the Mandarin is actually an invention of Aldrich Killian, founder and general director of AIM (Advanced Mechanical Ideas), to mask his illegal activities as terrorist attacks. Killian conspires with the United States' vice president to manipulate both sides of the war on terror to his own benefit. Killian is an American citizen with an Irish surname—not exactly an Eastern enemy. A rising sense of urgency is framing China–US relations in unavoidably conflictive terms, equating rising power with hostile power. Allison (2017) called it the "Thucydides Trap"[41]: when an established great power finds itself faced with a rising state, tensions rise as the new power displaces the old. Of the sixteen cases of transition of power since the late fifteenth century, twelve resulted in war. China's economic expansion and power growth challenge American hegemony just like a rising Athens defied an established Sparta. That is why Washington sees China as Fu Manchu. China's quest for status as a risen power would clash with that of the United States to remain in the lead.

Beijing sees itself more as Shang-Chi, who seeks peace and harmony in a weary world while opposing those who would tear it down. He is also the son of Fu Manchu, although raised completely unaware of his father's evil pursuits. The name Shang-Chi means "emergence and advancing of the spirit." This advancement is reflected both in the comic and in the long-term Chinese narrative of its path in world affairs. Shang-Chi found himself tasked by the secret society he was inducted in to assassinate an old enemy of his father. However, during the mission, he came into contact with a "venerable" British secret agent Smith, who "illuminated" him, with what we can assume is the "light" of Western civilization. After agreeing to work with Smith to stop his father, Shang-Chi met Smith's agent Black Jack Tarr and MI-6 operative Clive Reston. Shang-Chi refused to formally join MI-6 but worked alongside the organization on many missions. According to the calculations of Angus Maddison (2007), from the birth of Jesus until the beginning of the nineteenth century, China and India represented half of the world's GDP and were more technologically innovative and advanced than Europe. The Chinese economy moved from the north to the south between the eighth and thirteenth centuries. From the tenth to the early fifteenth century, China's per capita income was higher than Europe's. Between the fifteenth and eighteenth centuries (here one can find a measure of how long global power transitions can take), China relinquished economic leadership to Europe, which was entering modern capitalism. China and India plummeted between the beginning of the eighteenth century and the end of the twentieth century. Why? It can be attributed to a multiplicity of international factors: the Industrial Revolution in Europe, the formation of the United States of America, the decline of China during the Ming and Qing dynasties, and the expansion of British imperialism. Between 1820 and 1949, there was a long period of economic decline and "humiliation" from abroad. Despite the ravages of the Great Leap Forward (1958–1960), the Cultural Revolution (1966–1976), and the country's isolation and tensions with the USSR and the United States, China's GDP tripled between 1952 and 1978. Per capita income increased by 82 percent, labor productivity by 52 percent, and the share of industry in GDP rose from one-seventh of agriculture to roughly the same. During the reform period to a market economy promoted by Deng Xiaoping in 1978 and until 2003, GDP increased seven times and real per capita income five times. According to the national poverty line, the extreme poverty rate fell from 97.5 percent in 1978 to 1.7 percent in 2019. An average annual growth of 9.5 percent between 1978 and 2018 lifted 740 million people out of poverty, approximately the population of the state of New York per year. Chinese growth shifted the center of gravity of the world economy from the North Atlantic to Eurasia and the Pacific at a speed of approximately one hundred kilometers per year (Quah, 2011). In China's own words, it is a "nation standing firm in the east, facing a brilliant future of great rejuvenation. The long-cherished dream and aspiration of the Chinese people will surely become a reality." Its newfound international status is neither new nor a change. Rather, it is a return to the center, to what historically was the normalcy of world affairs.[42]

Chapter Twenty

Is Russia Like the Hulk?

Dr. Bruce Banner lives caught between the gentle scientist and the uncontrollable green monster driven by his anger that emerged after being exposed to a gamma ray experiment. Banner is cerebral while his alter ego the Hulk is a completely physical phenomenon. Today, the Russian Federation does not have the means to compete for world supremacy or balance American power like the USSR did during the four decades following World War II. In the 1950s, the Soviet Union was leading the way in the Cold War. In November 1956, leader Nikita Khrushchev—a true foreign-policy Hulk—told several Western ambassadors at a reception at the Polish embassy in Moscow: "We will bury you." By 1990, Gorbachev was proclaiming—more along the lines of Banner—that "peace means the rise from simple coexistence to cooperation and common creativity among countries and nations." After losing the Cold War to the United States, Russia retreated. Like Hulk after being quickly subdued by Thanos, there was a subsequent refusal to physically manifest himself, even as Bruce Banner continues the fight against him. The USSR disintegrated, leaving behind a significantly weaker Russia: three-quarters of the former Union's territory, half its population, half its economy, and a third of its military personnel. By 2021, Russia's economy was one-fifth of that of the United States and one-sixth of that of China at only 3 percent of global GDP. It is mostly an exporter of energy and commodities. Energy is the backbone of the Russian economy: oil accounts for 20 percent of Russia's GDP and 60 percent of total exports. However, as the green behemoth possesses the greatest raw strength of any natural being on Earth, Russia still has the largest total number of nuclear warheads: 6,375 as of May 2021. Nuclear power, oil and gas, cyber capabilities, proximity to Europe, and the potential of its alliance with China certainly give Moscow an international relations capacity to *smash*!

Banner transforms into the Hulk during moments of stress, anxiety, and, above all, anger. The change can be reversed if he reaches a state of calm, either by self-control or by romantic inspiration (the look of his beloved colleague Betty Ross or the special mantra used by Natasha Romanoff/Black Widow). This "reversion to Banner" is what many liberals expected—and still expect—from Russia. Historically, Western democratic expectations were placed on tsarist reformers, Soviet rulers, and the first term of President Vladimir Putin. Reformers aspire to a Russia eager to become like them. This is a form of Western narcissism that has repeatedly led to confusing institutional collapse with liberalization. Russia is fundamentally different from the West and geographically different from Europe. The Hulk is also different from the rest of the Avengers. Europe is maritime (no one lives more than 650 kilometers from the sea), and Russia is essentially landlocked. Ports in the Arctic Ocean are frozen over, and ports in the Black Sea and Baltic Sea can be blocked by enemies controlling straits. Thus, opportunities for international trade or even internal development are limited.[43] Energy is the critical revenue to fund the state budget (40 percent of it comes from oil and natural gas). It also funds military modernization. So Russia needs to consolidate its leverage over energy-importing countries, both to increase market share and to circumvent natural isolation by constructing natural gas pipelines, such as Nord Stream2 (to Germany), Turk Stream (to Turkey and southeastern Europe), and Power of Siberia (to China). Hulk's skin can resist damage from heavy weaponry, natural elements, and even unnatural ones. The country has also experienced that war is always a possibility, and that the greatest defense was the strategic depth. The Swedes, the French, and, on two occasions, the Germans taught them this.

Anger is central because it is the catalyst for periodic transformations. The Hulk is the embodiment of intense emotion and unresolved conflict within the Banner psyche (Rosenberg and Canzoneri, 2008). When Banner is threatened or strongly provoked, the green giant emerges to take charge of the situation and eradicate the danger. Just as Europe fears nationalism, Russia fears weakness. Moscow legitimately considers itself a great global power and a civilizational pole that has been marginalized and excluded from the liberal international order. But is it trying to destroy that order? Is it a "revenge power" that seeks to tear down the foundations of the liberal world order? Or is it a "defensive power" that works for incremental modifications within the existing order? Some analysts see Moscow focused mainly on reclaiming Russia's status as a great power, while others argue Russian foreign policy is centered on protecting the country's status as the dominant power in the post-Soviet region and defending against foreign interference in the country's domestic affairs. A third view contends Russia is an "aggressive isolationist." This is in line with the *Hulkean* tradition[44] and would explain the aggressiveness and expansionism in foreign policy as unresolved conflicts within the Russian polis. Russia's foreign policy priorities traditionally have focused on the post-Soviet region and the West, including relations and tensions with NATO, the United States, and Europe. However, Russia under President Vladimir Putin (like the Soviet Union) also pursues a global foreign policy. As relations with its neighbors and Western countries have become more adversarial, Russia has sought to balance against Western powers and interests. Bruce Banner spent five years hiding from the US army in Brazil and then went into hiding again in India. President Vladimir Putin's regime would deliberately play a destabilizing role in international affairs to boost its internal legitimacy. Russia defies the world order, it is true, but it mostly frames its actions within the existing international normative framework. Although it complains about and obstructs the liberal order (sovereignty vs. intervention, pluralism vs. universality, US hegemony vs. multipolar equilibrium), Moscow presents no alternative vision.

Hulk as a superhero is the same as Russia as an international power: it has no plan to fight evil or save the world. Its heroic aspects are by-products of what happens when it feels threatened. That is why it seeks to advance a "polycentric" world (Gromyko, 2015) where it can make its weight felt. Russia is projecting outward a narrative that seeks to reinforce its international prestige. According to the document that guides Russian foreign policy (MFARF, 2016), the country's strategic priority is to "preserve and improve its position in the world hierarchy of powers and responsibilities." Russia also promotes multilateral legal and institutional restrictions on the other most powerful actors as a means to ensure that Russia remains in the global Big League. Is Russia today a strong centralized state that has returned as a world power, competing with the United States for influence and allied with China to try to create a non-Western global order?[45] Or is it a declining empire that refuses to accept its reduced influence?[46] There is evidence of Russian use of force and military power projection in Georgia, Ukraine, Syria, and the Arctic, cyber-interference in the 2016 US presidential elections, fake news distribution operations in Europe, and alleged targeted overseas attacks against political opponents. The Hulk and Banner are one as Russia is strong and weak. Back in 1939, Winston Churchill knew something about Russia that Banner could affirm of the Hulk: it is as "a riddle, wrapped in a mystery, inside an enigma."

Chapter Twenty-One

Latin America's Eternal Return

Life as you now live it and have lived it, you will have to live once more and innumerable times more; and there will be nothing new in it, but every pain and every joy, every thought and sigh and everything unspeakably small or great in your life will have to return to you, all in the same succession and sequence.

At the center of Friedrich Nietzsche's philosophy is this idea of eternal return. All events in the world repeat themselves in the same sequence through an eternal series of cycles.[47] Juan Salvo is the Eternaut, the Argentine hero imagined by Germán Oesterheld and drawn by Francisco Solano López who resists an alien invasion from Buenos Aires. He presents a radically different model from the American classic superhero. He is not a superhero, for he has no special powers. He is not even a hero in the Greek sense of Heracles. He is a man rising to his best and attempting to overcome the odds reality has set against him. He does not achieve victory by vanquishing enemies with superpowers. He accomplishes survival by means of collective bonds of solidarity.

The Coriolis effect caused by the Earth's rotation is responsible for air being pulled to the right (counterclockwise) in the Northern Hemisphere and to the left (clockwise) in the Southern Hemisphere. The same happens when explaining superheroes as examples of international relations. The Economic Commission for Latin America and the Caribbean (ECLAC) affirmed the world had a periphery-center structure. This created a specific "peripheral" pattern of integration into the global economy, which consisted of producing goods and services for which there was little growth in international demand and importing goods and services for which the internal demand was rapidly expanding. At the same time, peripheral countries assimilate consumption patterns and technologies that were appropriate for the center but often unsuited to the availability of resources and the income level of the periphery. The main concern of the dominant theoretical schools of international relations (which we have already analyzed in the chapters on the JLA, Batman, Harvey Dent, and *Red Son*) is order, domination, or hegemony. But for a peripheral region like Latin America, the organizing concept of its own international experiences is autonomy. The Eternaut is not born a superhero; he makes himself a hero by rising up to the occasion. This school of international relations thought indigenous to Latin America had its prime exponent in Raúl Prebisch (1978), who posited that the existence of an inherently hierarchical world economic system made it impossible to analyze developing countries without considering their position within the international division of labor of the world economy. Alongside the Eternaut, there are a series of creatures invading Earth: giant beetles (Cascarudos); giant, armored, elephant-like beasts capable of knocking buildings down (Gurbos); humans captured and altered (robot-men); and humanoid species with many more fingers than humans, especially on their right hands (Manos or "Hands"). Ultimately, they are revealed to be "peripheral," pawns remotely controlled through implants by the real invaders (the center). The Ellos ("Them") are unseen creatures who remain hidden, controlling everything from the distance. Dependency theory (Cardoso and Faletto, 1967; Dos Santos, 1969; Sunkel, 1980) further addresses underdevelopment as a direct product of the expansion of the world capitalist system and dependency as a result of relations of subordination concocted by the elites of the global center. Those elites have an asymmetrical alliance with the dominant groups of the periphery, reminiscent of how the Them subdue the Manos: through implanting in them a "fear gland." In the 1969, politically charged version of the Eternaut, the alien invasion was not planet-wide: the powers had made a pact with the invader to surrender the Third World in exchange for not being attacked.

Latin America suffers from problems that seem to have an eternal return: underdevelopment (economic), dependence (technological), foreign debt (38 percent of the debt over the GDP but with cases like Argentina that reach 53 percent), employment (8 percent of unemployment, 48.5 percent of informal sector employment), poverty (30 percent and 10.5 percent of extreme poverty, more than 100 million poor people in the region), inequality (0.46 in the Gini coefficient[48]), and weakness (institutional and military). These are historical and structural characteristics of these societies that seem to be maintained even in periods of growth and prosperity. Granted, there are some encouraging trends: the region has ceased to be the most unequal continent in the world in terms of income, overtaken by the Middle East (Darvas, 2019). It is a "zone of peace," free of nuclear weapons, with no interstate wars between neighbors since 1883. It also has no major sectarian violence or ethnic or religious strife. At the same time, the region is home to forty-one of the fifty most dangerous cities in the world, has a homicide rate of 22 per

100,000 inhabitants (four times the world average), and accounts for 39 percent of global homicides (despite representing 9 percent of the global population).

Internally, Guillermo O'Donnell (1972) demonstrated how in Latin America a "dependent" economic modernization did not produce the expected favorable conditions for democracy. Much to the contrary, it favored the emergence of bureaucratic-authoritarian repressive regimes. The author of the Eternaut himself was assassinated for the political impact his comic had. More recently, the region has experienced a democratic expansion without historical precedent.[49] Today it is the region with the third-highest proportion of democracies (86 percent), after North America (100 percent) and Europe (93 percent). Of the twenty-two countries in Latin America and the Caribbean covered by the Global State of Democracy, nineteen are democracies, one is a hybrid regime (Nicaragua), and two are autocracies (Cuba and Venezuela).[50] For Mancur Olson (1965), coercion or inducements must be present in order for a group of rational, self-interested individuals to act in their common interest. This "zero contribution" thesis has limits to what can be empirically observed. Ostrom (2000) pointed out its limits from the perspective of economics—and Oesterheld (2007) from comic books. "We are Robinsons; this house is our island," says Salvo in one of the first vignettes. When the first stage of the alien invasion—the deadly snow—ensues, the four friends who were gathered for a card game (Salvo, Favalli, Herbert, and Polsky) have initial individual reactions. This costs Polsky his life, who dies crossing the street to return home. Similarly, the individual responses of Latin American states to globalization, economic development, and democratic consolidation have delivered very limited success. In the case of the Eternaut, the fight against an interstellar enemy makes it possible to unite everyone in a common destiny. "Everyone" has a radical bias for the writer. The survivors are very symbolic: Juan Salvo and his family, Favalli (a physicist, symbol of the belief in scientific progress), Mosca (the historian, the symbol of Latin America's need to connect to its own roots), Pablo (the symbol of youth, change, hope, possibility), Franco (the worker, the people whom Oesterheld praises as the "true hero of history"). The eternal return of the Eternaut in successive editions through the years and an announced Netflix series keep bringing to the fore the international dilemmas of Latin America while inviting us to imagine a different future. The region cannot be a rule-maker in a volatile, turbulent, and increasingly competitive and conflictive world. Individual countries will be relegated to rule-takers at best. At worst, they will be rule-breakers. Together, they can aspire to being rule-shapers to protect the region's autonomy. This is the conceptual basis for Latin American regional integration initiatives, personified in the character of Juan Salvo. Oesterheld writes about it at the end of the prologue: "Now that I think about it, it occurs to me that perhaps because of this lack of a central hero, The Eternaut is one of my favorite stories. The true hero of is a collective hero, a human group. Even though I did not mean it that way, it reflected my intimate feeling: the only valid hero is the collective hero, never the individual hero."

Chapter Twenty-Two

Epilogue

Bane's Face Mask

This book is being written while the world is in global quarantine because of the COVID-19 pandemic. Bane is very representative of what has happened during this time of pandemic—and not just because he wears a face mask. He was born in a prison, just as there was speculation that the virus had been produced in a laboratory. When Bane returns to Santa Prisca prison, he questions the Jesuit priest who had educated him about his origins. The monk explains there were four men who could possibly have been his father: a local revolutionary, an American doctor (whom Bane mistakenly thinks is Thomas Wayne), an English mercenary, and a Swiss banker. It was the same with the origin of the SARS-CoV-2 virus. By mid-2021, theories of accidental release from a lab and zoonotic spillover both remained viable. In a 2021 letter to *Nature*, a group of scientists called for a proper investigation that should be transparent, objective, data-driven, inclusive of broad expertise, subject to independent oversight, and responsibly managed to minimize the impact of conflicts of interest. Those conflicts of interest are directly determined by the issues we have reviewed in this book. The pandemic exacerbated the existing geopolitical competition, heightened the competition for profit from multinational corporations, sparked ethical and economic debates over vaccine distribution, and provoked a war of misinformation. In *The Mysterious Stranger*, Mark Twain writes: "Statesmen will invent cheap lies, putting the blame upon the nation that is attacked, and every man will be glad of those conscience-soothing falsities, and will diligently study them, and refuse to examine any refutations of them; and thus he will by and by convince himself that the war is just, and will thank God for the better sleep he enjoys after this process of grotesque self-deception." The superpower of an academic is to try to shed light on knowledge to help as many as possible to avoid the complacency of self-deception.

While Bane is looking for his probable Swiss father in Rome, he meets Talia al Ghul, who introduces him to her father, the infamous terrorist Ra's al Ghul. Bane so impresses the mysterious leader that he is anointed his heir, an "honor" he had previously imparted to Bruce Wayne.[51] What impact will the pandemic have on great-power relations and on the structure of globalization? Will it deepen continuity or accelerate change? Over the past ten thousand years, human societies have evolved from small-scale egalitarian groups to complex, large-scale societies characterized by great differentials in wealth and power, extensive division of labor, and elaborate governance structures. Like ecosystems or the human immune system, world order is a complex adaptive system, with many agents that are acting and reacting to each other's behavior. Multiple interconnected elements recombine in ways that cannot be traced linearly nor predicted in advance. Bane is addicted to Venom (which makes him wear his face mask constantly). After his recovery, he falls back. He is an ally of Batman and then his enemy. Batman saves his life in the Lazarus Pit, and Bane breaks his back and leaves him a paraplegic. There are effects that we cannot predict today even if we have identified the main components and trends. For the future of international relations, when a system receives a shock, it is impossible to anticipate the final outcome. It could be a marginal modification or complete collapse due to cumulative cascade effects. New "emergent" properties arise from interactions that were not present in the initial elements. We are going through a particularly volatile time in the international system that increases systemic instability, enhanced by the increasing speed and scope of global interconnections.

As coronaviruses jump from bats to pangolins and humans, they evolve and recombine. Viruses change form as a strategy to increase the chances of survival. As with Bane, the pandemic prevented a clear-cut distinction between human and nonhuman: we are immersed in an infinitely radiating network of viruses, bats, rainforests, humans, trafficking, markets, airplanes, face masks, nation-states, borders, geopolitics, and back. From the microscopic to the macrosocial, we have been pulled back forcefully into nature, reminding us of our place in a great chain of beings. The spread of the COVID-19 virus shows that changes quickly escalate into crises, which are rapidly transmitted and have spillover and multiplier effects on other areas (employment, security, debt, inflation) in unpredictable directions and orders of magnitude. For instance, in Christopher Nolan's *Batman: The Dark Knight Rises* (2012), Bane seeks only personal revenge. In the process, he also becomes a nuclear terrorist and fosters class struggle within Gotham.

Notes

1. The "separation" is divided into: (1) "the call of adventure" (signs of the hero's vocation), (2) "the refusal of the call" (escape or denial), (3) "supernatural help" (unexpected assistance for those who have undertaken the right adventure), (4) "the crossing of the first threshold," and (5) "the belly of the whale" (the passage to the kingdom of night). "Initiation" consists of six divisions: (1) "the way of trials" (of the dangerous aspect), (2) "the encounter with the goddess" (childhood recovered), (3) "woman as temptation" (sin and agony), (4) "reconciliation with the father," (5) "apotheosis," and (6) "ultimate grace." Finally, "return" is: (1) "the refusal to return," (2) "the magic escape," (3) "the rescue of the outside world," (4) "the crossing of the threshold of return" (return to the normal world), (5) "the possession of the two worlds," and (6) "freedom to live."

2. *Illegal Logging, Fishing, and Wildlife Trade: The Costs and How to Combat it*, World Bank, October 2019.

3. *Illicit Trade: Converging Criminal Networks*, Organization for Economic Cooperation and Development, April 2016.

4. *Digital in 2020*, HootSuite, available at https://wearesocial.com/digital-2020.

5. The "psychopathology of hypercapitalism" is the exploitation of the most beloved and intimate relations of human beings for the benefit of a giant American company (Facebook) that has become the dominant way of organizing communications.

6. *Freedom on the Net 2019*, Freedom House, available at https://www.freedomonthenet.org/sites/default/files/2019-11/11042019_Report_FH_FOTN_2019_final_Public_Download.pdf.

7. *Cyborg, 2*(18), January 2018, DC Comics.

8. In Latin America, Bogotá and Lima reached ten million, joining the four pre-existing mega-cities in the region: Buenos Aires, Mexico City, Rio de Janeiro, and São Paulo.

9. The UN adopted the term *transnational corporations* in 1995, defining them as "enterprises that own or control production or service facilities outside the country in which they are based."

10. A cube-shaped crystalline containment vessel containing the Space Stone, one of the six Infinity Stones created before the universe and possessing unlimited energy.

11. Acronym for Strategic Homeland Intervention, Enforcement, and Logistics Division, which in the Marvel universe is the intelligence, espionage, and antiterrorism agency born in the United States after the Second World War to fight HYDRA and then evolving as a protector of planetary security under the command of the World Security Council.

12. One kiloton is the equivalent of 1,000 tons of TNT.

13. The Manhattan Project was the code name for the secret US project to develop a nuclear weapon during World War II. Its main outcome was the Little Boy and Fat Man bombs dropped on Hiroshima and Nagasaki in August 1945. Although named for one of the five metropolitan districts that make up New York City, most of the work was done in Los Alamos, New Mexico.

14. This phenomenon exists in reality and is called Cherenkov radiation. If Manhattan were leaking high-energy electrons, it would create a blue glow around him. And presumably, if it changed the speed of the electrons, it would even change how dark the blue was, as in the television studio in the book.

15. Nuclear bombs are fission bombs: they split the nucleus of an atom and when the neutrons in the atom split, they hit the nuclei of nearby atoms, splitting them up in a highly explosive chain reaction as well. Thermonuclear bombs have more power because an ignition explosion compresses the sphere of plutonium-239, which will then undergo fission. Inside the plutonium pit, there is a hydrogen gas chamber. The high temperatures and pressures created by fission cause the hydrogen atoms to fuse. This fusion process releases neutrons, which feed back into the plutonium-239, dividing more atoms and driving the fission chain reaction.

16. In February 2004, Abdul Qadeer Khan, the "father" of the Pakistani nuclear weapon, admitted that he had transferred sensitive nuclear technology to Libya, Iran, and North Korea.

17. In 2017, South Korea's National Intelligence Service (NIS) estimated that the total cost of the North Korean nuclear weapon was between 1.1 and 3.2 billion dollars.

18. R. M. Rilke, "First Elegy," in *Duino elegies and the sonnets to Orpheus* (New York: Houghton Mifflin Harcourt, 2005).

19. Despite having given US$36 billion in Amazon shares to his ex-wife MacKenzie, Bezos is the world's richest person for the third year running, with a net value in 2020 of US$142 billion. The global COVID-19 pandemic only benefited Amazon because of increased demand from consumers who stayed at home and shopped online. On July 20, 2020, Bezos's fortune increased by US$13 billion in one day.

20. For several years, the magazine calculated the net worth of the richest characters in novels, films, television, and games; built portfolios based on those stories; and valued them using real-world commodities and stock prices. The latest is available at https://www.forbes.com/sites/davidewalt/2013/07/31/the-2013-forbes-fictional-15/.

21. In May 2019, the International Commission on Stratigraphy (which establishes the Earth's geological eras) voted to date the beginning of the Anthropocene in the mid-twentieth century because of the rapidly growing human population, the rapid pace of industrial production, the use of agricultural chemicals, and the first atomic bomb explosions, which covered the world with radioactive waste that became embedded in sediments and glacial ice and thus became part of the geological record. This geological time marker would signal the end of the Holocene and the beginning of the Anthropocene. The formal proposal will be raised in 2021.

22. Thirteen million metric tons of plastic are dumped into the ocean each year, and plastic debris kills one million seabirds and other ocean wildlife annually. Ocean acidification from fossil fuel dumping reduces the ability of crustaceans to form and destroys species such as coral. Meanwhile, global warming makes ocean water less hospitable to plankton and algae, the basis of the entire marine food web. Because of threats like these, scientists fear that the ocean is facing a mass extinction event.

23. In the North Pacific floats a continent of rubbish that they call "the great rubbish stain of the Pacific." According to estimates by Carlos Plankton of the Institute of Marine Life in Morro Bay, California, it measures some 1.6 million km^2 (three times the size of France) and contains 80,000 tons of plastic, 94 percent of which is made up of small plastic fragments eroded from larger pieces.

24. Slavoj Zizek quotes a speech in which Bolivian president Evo Morales states: "Capitalism is the source of asymmetries and imbalances in the world" and proposes to restore "natural" balance and symmetry. For Zizek, the environmentalist/indigenist discourse attacks and rejects the modern subjectivity that destroys the traditional cosmology of Mother Earth and Father Sky.

25. The comic's reference to Thomas Malthus is as clear as it is informative. In 1798, he wrote *An Essay on the Principle of Population*. In it, Malthus raised doubts about whether a nation could ever reach a point where laws would no longer be required and in which everyone lived prosperously

and harmoniously, a declared aim of the Lantern Corps. He warned that while population would grow geometrically (by factors of four, eight, and sixteen), food resources would grow only in arithmetical (by factors of three, four, five, and so on) proportion. There was no hope food supply could keep up: clearing new land for farming or improving the yields of crops could never match unchecked population growth. This creates the conditions for a long-term shortage that would lead inevitably to famine and misery. The principles had great influence on Darwin's and Wallace's thinking about the "struggle for life" as the source of natural selection of the "fittest."

26. The Earth is the only exception to the rule as it had four Green Lanterns: Hal Jordan, Kyle Rayner, John Stewart, and Guy Gardner. There is also a fifth Green Lantern on Earth who has never belonged to the Corps: Alan Scott.

27. On May 11, 2020, a Chinese rocket landed in the Atlantic Ocean. The rocket's empty central platform weighed nearly eighteen tons and was the largest piece of space debris to fall to Earth since 1991.

28. The term *regional hegemon* refers to a country that is so powerful in relation to the other countries in its region that it can dominate affairs in that region and force other countries in that region to support (or not oppose) its own political and economic objectives. For example, the United States established itself in the nineteenth century as the hegemon in the Americas.

29. On the cover of *Captain America*'s issue number 1, he is seen punching Hitler in the face.

30. These are elements of a discourse of identity that inevitably is based on distinctions between "self" and "other." The identity of the EU as a normative power (Venus) is contrasted with that of the United States as a military power (Mars). But the United States has been one of the biggest promoters of norms in the international system for decades. Indeed, the great hegemonic powers always tend to build the system according to their own principles, norms, and rules. Nazi Germany, the Soviet Union, the United States, the EU—all have used the rule-power continuum.

31. "Hard" or material power is constituted by military capability and industrial/economic development. Joseph Nye called *soft power* the ability to persuade others in the international system to want to be like you. It is a power of attraction rather than imposition.

32. There are gases that produce the greenhouse effect. The largest is carbon dioxide (CO^2), but there are others such as nitrous oxide (N^2O), methane (CH^4), and ozone (O^3) and halocarbons, hydrofluorocarbons (HFCs), and perfluorocarbons (PFCs). Being carbon neutral implies carrying out an annual inventory of the sources of greenhouse gas emissions and taking action to reduce, offset, and/or remove emissions with the aim that the total net amount in tons of CO^2 released during the year minus the tons reduced, offset, or removed results in zero.

33. The IMF also has the classification of "low-income developing countries" (LIDC). These are countries that have per capita income levels below a certain threshold (currently set at US$2,700), structural characteristics consistent with limited development and structural transformation, and insufficient external financial linkages to be considered emerging market economies. See: https://www.imf.org/external/pubs/ft/weo/faq.htm#q4b.

34. The World Bank assigns the world's economies to four income groups—low, lower-middle, upper-middle, and high-income countries. The classifications are updated each year on July 1 and are based on GNI per capita in current USD (using the Atlas method exchange rates) of the previous year.

35. Available at https://www.wto.org/english/tratop_e/devel_e/d1who_e.htm. Other members may question the decision.

36. In October 2019, the United States Department of Agriculture (USDA) listed Wakanda as a partner under a free trade agreement with the United States. It was added to the list by accident during a database test. The USDA's online tariff search engine showed a detailed list of goods apparently traded by the two nations, including ducks, donkeys, and dairy cows.

37. In the comic, Wakanda has fiercely guarded its borders against invasions by neighboring tribes, nineteenth-century European mercenaries, and Nazis. The fantasy of an African nation untouched by colonial influence may have been based on Lesotho, which was able to resist the Zulus and Boers and was only slightly colonized by the United Kingdom.

38. Argentina, Australia, Brazil, Canada, China, France, Germany, India, Indonesia, Italy, Japan, Mexico, Russia, Saudi Arabia, South Africa, Turkey, South Korea, the United Kingdom, the United States, and the European Union.

39. After withdrawing 19.6 million toys manufactured in China with lead paint, Mattel officially admitted on August 14, 2007, that "the vast majority of products that were recalled were the result of a Mattel design flaw, not a manufacturing flaw by China's partners."

40. See in this respect the differentiation established by the World Health Organization at https://www.who.int/emergencies/diseases/novel-coronavirus-2019/technical-guidance/naming-the-coronavirus-disease-(covid-2019)-and-the-virus-that-causes-it.

41. The Greek historian explained the Peloponnesian War in the fifth century BC by the rise of Athens to greatness and the fear that this provoked in Sparta (Hanson, 1998).

42. The name of China in Chinese is 中国 or Zhōngguó. The first character means "center or middle" and the second "country, nation or kingdom." China calls itself "the middle kingdom."

43. In Central Asia, Russia has led security and trade blocs such as the Collective Security Treaty Organization (CSTO) with Armenia, Belarus, Ka-

zakhstan, Kyrgyzstan, and Tajikistan or the Eurasian Economic Union (EAEU) with Armenia, Belarus, and Kazakhstan.

44. In *The Incredible Hulk* (2008), Banner exiles himself to Brazil. In *The Avengers* (2012), he secretly resides in India. In *Avengers: Age of Ultron* (2015), still in the form of the Hulk, he escapes to an unknown destination in an uncommunicated quinjet. In *Thor: Ragnarok* (2017), he is once again in self-exile as a gladiator in the Grand Master's arena on the planet Sakaar. And after being almost completely absent in *Avengers: Infinity War* (2018), the Hulk is back in *Avengers: Endgame* (2019), already with Bruce Banner fully able to master his transformation without losing control. This is the image Western liberals want of Russia.

45. A closer look reveals that relations between China and Russia are based on a mutual fear of American containment. The strategic partnership seeks to counter US influence and promote economic growth. As the weaker partner in the relation, Russia will continue to have concerns about China's strategic intentions.

46. Declining powers can be even more dangerous. On their downward trajectory, they undertake riskier actions as they perceive they have less to lose, like the Austro-Hungarian Empire in 1914.

47. The texts are difficult to interpret since all the expositions of Nietzsche's thought on the concept are presented in an elliptical and allusive manner or in hypothetical terms (*The Gay Science*, 1882) or in highly metaphorical and quasi-hermetic terms (*Thus Spoke Zarathustra*, 1885).

48. The Gini coefficient measures the inequality of income distribution in a country. A Gini coefficient of 0 represents perfect equality, while a coefficient of 1 implies the highest levels of inequality.

49. The "third wave of democratization" (Huntington, 1991) began in the region in 1978 with the Dominican Republic. It was followed by Ecuador (1979); Peru (1980); Honduras (1982); Argentina (1983); El Salvador (1984); Bolivia, Brazil, and Uruguay (all in 1985); Guatemala (1986); Paraguay (1989); Chile, Nicaragua, and Panama (all in 1990); and Mexico (2000).

50. For Latin America and the Caribbean, it covers twenty-two of the twenty-nine countries in the region, as only countries with more than one million inhabitants are included in the sample. This is Cuba, Dominican Republic, Haiti, Jamaica, and Trinidad and Tobago in the Caribbean; Costa Rica, El Salvador, Guatemala, Honduras, Mexico, Nicaragua, and Panama in Central America; and Argentina, Bolivia, Brazil, Chile, Colombia, Ecuador, Paraguay, Peru, Uruguay, and Venezuela in South America.

51. Ra's al Ghul and Bane launch a plague attack on Gotham, which Batman avoids. He also defeats Bane and is thus even after his previous match in which Bane had broken his spine (*Batman*, No. 497, 1993).

Index

References

Allison, G. (2017). *Destined for war: Can America and China escape Thucydides's trap?* New York: Houghton Mifflin Harcourt.

Allison, G. (2018). "Nuclear terrorism." *PRISM, 7*(3), 2–21.

Auty, Richard M. (1994). "Industrial policy reform in six large newly industrializing countries: The resource curse thesis." *World Development, 22*(1), 11–26.

Bourguignon, F., B. Milanovic, and P. Belser et al. (2016). "Inequalities: Many intersecting dimensions." *World Social Science Report.* Paris: ISSC, IDS, and UNESCO.

Brodie, B., F. S. Dunn, A. Wolfers et al. (1946). "The absolute weapon: Atomic power and world order." *American Journal of International Law, 40*(4).

Campbell, J. (1959). *El Héroe de las mil caras.* Ciudad de México: Fondo de Cultura Económica.

Cardoso, F., and E. Faletto. (1967). *Dependencia y desarrollo en América Latina. Ensayo de interpretación sociológica.* Ciudad de México: Siglo XXI.

Castells, M. (January 29, 2011). "La wikirrevolución del jazmín." *La Vanguardia.* http://www.lavanguardia.com/opinion/ articulos/20110129/54107291983/index.html#ixzz2Or6e3LAW.

Clausewitz, C. V. (1976). *On war* (trans. M. Howard and P. Paret). Princeton, NJ: Princeton University Press.

Coffey, C., P. Espinoza Revollo, and R. Harvey et al. (2020). *Time to care.* Oxfam Briefing Paper. London: Oxfam International.

Cooper, R. (2000). *The post-modern state and the world order.* London: Demos.

Darvas, Z. (2019). "Global interpersonal income inequality decline: The role of China and India." *World Development, 121*, 16–32.

Diamond, L. (2002). "Elections without democracy: Thinking about hybrid regimes." *Journal of Democracy, 13*(2), 21–35.

Dos Santos, T. (1969). "El nuevo carácter de la dependencia." *Cuadernos del Centro de Estudios Sociológicos, 10*, 1–25.

Drezner, Daniel W. (2014). *Theories of international politics and zombies.* Princeton, NJ: Princeton University Press.

Duchêne, F. (1972). "Europe's role in world peace." In R. Mayne (ed.), *Europe tomorrow: Sixteen Europeans look ahead.* London: Fontana/Collins.

Dunlap, R. E., and A. M. McCright. (2011). "Organized climate change denial." *The Oxford Handbook of Climate Change and Society, 1*, 144–60.

Fitzgerald, J., D. Leblang, and J. C. Teets. (2014). "Defying the law of gravity: The political economy of international migration." *World Politics, 66*(3), 406–45.

Forster, P., L. Forster, C. Renfrew, and M. Forster. (2020). "Phylogenetic network analysis of SARS-CoV-2 genomes." *Proceedings of the National Academy of Sciences, 117*(17), 9241–43.

Foucault, Michel. (1977). *Discipline and punish: The birth of the prison.* (trans. A. Sheridan). New York: Vintage.

Foucault, Michel. (1980). "Two Lectures." In Colin Gordon (ed.), *Power/Knowledge: Selected interviews and other writings, 1972–1977.* New York: Pantheon.

Gitlin, T. (1979). "Prime time ideology: The hegemonic process in television entertainment." *Social Problems, 26*(3), 251–66.

Gromyko, A. (2015). "Russia-EU relations at a crossroads: Preventing a new Cold War in a polycentric world." *Southeast European and Black Sea Studies, 15*(2), 141–49.

Hanson, V. D. (1998). *The landmark Thucydides: A comprehensive guide to the Peloponnesian War.* New York: Simon and Schuster.

Hirschman, A. O. (1970). *Exit, voice, and loyalty: Responses to decline in firms, organizations, and states.* Cambridge, MA: Harvard University Press.

Hofstede, G. (2011). "Dimensionalizing cultures: The Hofstede model in context." *Online Readings in Psychology and Culture, 2*(1).

Huntington, S. P. (1991). *The third wave: Democratization in the late twentieth century.* Norman: University of Oklahoma Press.

Huntington, S. P. (2004). *Who are we? The challenges to America's national identity.* New York: Simon and Schuster.

Ikenberry, G. J. (1999). "Institutions, strategic restraint, and the persistence of American postwar order." *International Security, 23*(3), 43–78.

Jepperson, R. L., A. Wendt, and P. J. Katzenstein. (1996). "Norms, identity, and culture in national security." *The Culture of National Security: Norms and Identity in World Politics, 33,* 34.

Jervis, R. (1978). "Cooperation under the security dilemma." *World Politics, 30*(2), 167–214.

Jung, C. G. (1959). *The archetypes and the collective unconscious.* London: Routledge.

Kagan, R. (2004). *Of paradise and power: America and Europe in the new world order.* New York: Vintage Books.

Keohane, Robert O. (1988). "International institutions: Two approaches." *International Studies Quarterly, 32*(4), 379–96.

Lenton, T. M., H. Held, and E. Kriegler et al. (2008). "Tipping elements in the Earth's climate system." *Proceedings of the National Academy of Sciences, 105*(6), 1786–93.

Levitsky, S., and L. A. Way. (2002). "Elections without democracy: The rise of competitive authoritarianism." *Journal of Democracy, 13*(2), 51–65.

Maddison, A. (2007). *Chinese economic performance in the long run. Second edition, revised and updated: 960–2030 AD.* Paris: OECD.

Manners, I. (2006). "Normative power Europe reconsidered: beyond the crossroads." *Journal of European Public Policy, 13*(2), 182–99.

Marx, K. (1976). *Capital: A critique of political economy,* vol. 1. New York: Vintage Books.

Mead, W. R. (2004). "America's sticky power." *Foreign Policy, 141*(1), 46–53.

MFARF, Ministry of Foreign Affairs of the Russian Federation. (2016). Foreign Policy Concept of the Russian Federation, approved by President of the Russian Federation Vladimir Putin, November 30.

Milanovic, B. (2015). "Global inequality of opportunity: How much of our income is determined by where we live?" *Review of Economics and Statistics, 97*(2), 452–60.

Morozov, Evgeny. (2013). *To save everything, click here: The folly of technological solutionism.* New York: Public Affairs.

Nayak, M. (2015). *Who is worthy of protection? Gender-based asylum and U.S. immigration politics.* New York: Oxford University Press.

North, D. C. (1991). "Institutions." *Journal of Economic Perspectives, 5*(1): 97–112.

O'Donnell, G. A. (1972). "Modernización y golpes militares. Teoría, comparación y el caso argentino." *Desarrollo Económico, 12*(47): 519–66.

OECD. (2018). *Multinational enterprises in the global economy: Heavily debated but hardly measured.* https://www.oecd.org/industry/ind/MNEs-in-the-global-economy-policy-note.pdf.

Oesterheld, H. G., and F. Solano López. (2007). *El Eternauta: 1957–2007, 50 años.* Buenos Aires: Doedytores.

Olson, M. (1965). *The theory of collective action: Public goods and the theory of groups.* Cambridge, MA: Harvard University Press.

Ostrom, E. (2000). "Collective action and the evolution of social norms." *Journal of Economic Perspectives, 14*(3), 137–58.

Pierpauli, G. (April 25, 2011). "De las costas africanas a Europa." *Radio del Principado de Asturias.* https://www.youtube.com/watch?v=Js1hykatA6s.

Piketty, T. (2014). *Capital in the twenty-first century.* Cambridge, MA: Harvard University Press.

Prebisch, R. (1978). "Notas sobre el desarrollo del capitalismo periférico." *Estudios Internacionales, 11*(43), 3–25.

Quah, D. (2011). "The global economy's shifting centre of gravity." *Global Policy, 2*(1), 3–9.

Robinson, J. A., R. Torvik, and T. Verdier. (2006). "Political foundations of the resource curse." *Journal of Development Economics, 79*(2), 447–68.

Rockström, J., W. Steffen, and K. Noone et al. (2009). "Planetary boundaries: Exploring the safe operating space for humanity." *Ecology and Society, 14*(2).

Rolland, Nadège. (2020). "China's pandemic power play." *Journal of Democracy, 31*(3), 25–38.

Rosenberg, R. S., and J. Canzoneri (Eds.) (2008). *The psychology of superheroes: An unauthorized exploration.* Chicago: BenBella Books.

Ross, M. L. (1999). "The political economy of the resource curse." *World Politics, 51*(2), 297–322.

Rothkopf, D. (2008). *Superclass: The global power elite and the world they are making.* New York: Farrar, Straus and Giroux.

Rucka, G., D. Eaglesham, and R. Krissing. (March 2001). "The most suitable person." *President Luthor Secret Files and Origins 1.* New York: DC Comics.

Sachs, J. D., and A. M. Warner. (2001). "The curse of natural resources." *European Economic Review, 45*(4–6), 827–38.

Said, E. W. (1979). *Orientalism.* New York: Vintage Books.

Schlesinger, Arthur M. (1999). *The cycles of American history.* Boston: Houghton Mifflin.

SIPRI. (April 26, 2021). "World military spending rises to almost US$2 trillion in 2020." https://sipri.org/media/press-release/2021/world-military-spending-rises-almost-2-trillion-2020.

Steffen, W., R. A. Sanderson, and P. D. Tyson et al. (2005). *Global change and the earth system: A planet under pressure.* Berlin: Springer.

Sunkel, O. (1980). "El desarrollo de la teoría de la dependencia." *Transnacionalización y dependencia.* Madrid: Ediciones Cultura Hispánica del Instituto de Cooperación Iberoamericana.

United Nations Department of Economic and Social Affairs, Population Division. (2019). *The international migrant stock 2019.* Dataset. https://www.un.org/en/development/desa/population/migration/data/estimates2/estimates19.asp.

United Nations Department of Economic and Social Affairs, Population Division. (2019). *World urbanization prospects 2018* (ST/ESA/SER.A/421).

Vreeland, J. R. (2008). "The effect of political regime on civil war: Unpacking anocracy." *Journal of Conflict Resolution, 52*(3), 401–25.

Weyland, K. (1998). "The political fate of market reform in Latin America, Africa, and Eastern Europe." *International Studies Quarterly, 42*(4), 645–73.

Wildavsky, A. (1994). "Why self-interest means less outside of a social context: Cultural contributions to a theory of rational choices." *Journal of Theoretical Politics, 6*(2), 131–59.

Wright Mills, C. (1956). *The power elite.* New York: Oxford University Press.